PARADISE PRESERVES

Condiments of Hawaii

A COLLECTION OF KAMAAINA CONDIMENTS
With A Special Section On Curries

By Yvonne Neely Armitage

Drawings by
Lorna Armitage Cabato
and
Paul Douglas Armitage

 Press Pacifica

Library of Congress Cataloging-in-Publication Data

Armitage, Yvonne Neely.
    Pacific preserves.

    Includes index.
    1. Condiments   2. Cookery (Curry)   I. Title.
TX819.A1A76   1987   641.3'384   87-32710
ISBN 0-916630-63-3 (alk. paper)

Cover photo by Jane Wilkins Pultz

Manufactured in the United States of America by
Kingsport Press, Kingsport, Tennessee.
and typeset by The Last Word, Kailua, Hawaii.

Available from the publisher: Press Pacifica, P. O. Box 47
Kailua, Hawaii 96734

PARADISE
PRESERVES

Dedicated to the memory of my mother
Amelia Dell Neely
and to my children Lorna and Paul
who illustrated this book

For a malihini, born on a farm in Wisconsin, arriving in Hawaii on her way to the Orient in the early '20s and eventually marrying in Honolulu, my mother learned to cook a variety of Island favorites. She could make the biggest and tastiest laulaus anyone ever ate, but never learned to eat raw fish.

Moving to Lihue in the 1930s our family became a part of the large gatherings at Papalinahoa where the Sunday sailors collected after the yacht races in Nawiliwili harbor. The ladies cooked up vast amounts of food to serve the ravenous mob, while the children had soda pop fights and got in everyone's way. I recently found carefully penned recipes, in my mother's hand, for things like escalloped potatoes for 50 people and lists of every provision you would need to serve hamburgers and beans to a hundred hungry souls.

During the war years my mother turned our dining room at Kealia into a Red Cross bandage center and the neighborhood gathered to do their part for the war effort. She, like other Kauai housewives learned to do without certain staples not available after December 7th. Wartime housewives made mock apple pie from soda crackers, butter from coconut milk; and, cooked endless, dreary meatless meals. They could never disguise canned spinach which I loathe to this day!

Batch after batch of cookies were baked and passed out to the GIs on the Army patrols that went past our house in a never-ending parade of foot soldiers, jeeps, command cars, trucks, and weapons carriers. Our lanai was often heaped with bulky gasmasks, scarred metal helmets, stacked rifles and muddy fields boots which belonged to a few lonely soldiers invited in for a home cooked meal.

I'll never be the bountiful, tireless hostess my mother was, but my observations of her culinary efforts have given me a fine appreciation of good food and the pleasure gained from rattling around in my own kitchen and making glorious messes!

To her and all the Island hostesses whose entertaining I've enjoyed, this book is lovingly dedicated.

TABLE OF CONTENTS

Introduction

This collection of recipes for kamaaina condiments includes chutneys, fruit and vegetable pickles, relishes and sauces, a few marmalades, and a section on curry and the sambals, or side dishes served with curry. Most of the recipes herein are from a bulging, worn notebook I've kept for years, some are culled from clippings and adapted by me, others shared by friends, and all of them good!

I have never had any great success with making jams or jellies, I usually wind up with something that looks like road tar or an inferior grade of thin syrup that runs all over the place. I must have been eleven years old when I made my first jam with my playmate, Jane Frizelle Heine, at her house in Lihue. Jane's father was principal of Kauai High School, her mother taught history, and they were tolerant of our sometimes messy projects and the problems we created.

One day Jane and I had perched ourselves in the Java plum trees that lined the roadway coming up the hill from Nawiliwili to the campus. We had picked a sackfull of the purple, sour fruit and were happily pelting passing cars with them. Before we tired of the sport, some dear soul had reported us to a lone policeman on his beat, who came along and read us the riot act. We then spent the rest of the day making jam out of our ammunition. The Frizelle's stove burners were never the same after that, nor the pot we scorched the mess in, nor my mother's silver spoon she bent in half trying to get the dense, dark stuff out of the jar I took home.

I won't give you any recipes for guava jelly, but I will tell you about my uncle Bill who used to be the jellymaker in his family. Years ago when I was about five and my father was out of a job and broke, our family moved in with his sister Kathleen and her husband, Bill Beerman, and my three cousins, Joyce, Douggie and Bruce. Uncle Bill was superintendent of Hawaiian Pineapple cannery and lived atop Aiea Heights in what I remember as a rambling two-story white house on a large parcel of land. It took hours, so it seemed, to drive up that steep hill in our Model T. There were donkeys, dogs, cats, ducks, chickens and best of all, cousins for my brother, Dwight, and me to play with.

Sundays during guava season were the best when Uncle Bill loaded the old jalopy with cardboard boxes and we stood on the running boards, hanging on to the roof supports. He cranked up the machine and we'd drive off, dogs yapping behind us, into the wilds to search for ripe fruit. We made our own roads through the forests and shouted out whenever we spotted heavily laden trees. Uncle Bill would come to a stop. We'd pile off while he sat and rolled his Bull Durham with great ceremony to smoke unconcernedly as we clambered up the trees and filled the boxes with the hard, just-turning, greeny-yellow fruit which makes the best jelly.

Bee, as his wife called him, was a very proper, almost militant German who had been born at Kilauea on Kauai after his parents arrived from Bremen. A large number of German families had come to Hawaii to work on various sugar plantations. Uncle Bill had a great sense of humor, was a wonderful storyteller, fisherman, party-giver and jelly-maker and I loved him dearly.

His "kitchen" was outside under a huge mango tree, far away from the main house, his wife, kids and inlaws. It was *verboten* to go there unless you were invited! Two three-burner kerosene stoves were set up, large kettles brought out for the cooking, great sacks of sugar ripped open, knives sharpened to cut the fruit, and glass jars set to bubble in boiling pots. The smell of melting paraffin mingled with the scorching odor of guava juice as it sputtered and dribbled down the sides of the sticky kettles before it hit the hot burners. Hanging from tree limbs were clean muslin sacks tied up with steamy guava pulp, dripping pink juices into pans set under them.

Uncle Bill sat in an old chair, alternately dragging on a cigarette, taking a sip of his "kanaka high" and surveying the monumental task of putting out jar after jar of precious, clear, ruby-colored, perfect jelly. He had found an enviable way to embrace the bucolic setting and to forget for awhile the frantic, hot, noisy pace of the cannery. On a magnificent summer day he would let the soft breezes soothe him while he gazed at the view of Pearl Harbor and Ewa from his hilltop domain.

I guess that's what ruined me for every being able to make good jelly; how could I have that much fun!

CHUTNEY

CHUTNEY

I devour good chutney like good chocolate, greedily and with gusto! Some travelers to Hawaii and the Far East who are unaccustomed to the cuisine of Pacific and Asian cultures feel that chutney is merely a welcome coverup for some of the exotic tastes they encounter, a saving grace to avoid speculation on the actual ingredients of the strange dishes they are served. Chutneys are, to my taste, the most delectable of all condiments and I approach this sauce like a worshipper of the finer things in life, with respect and a great fondness for the incomparable taste of a supremely delicious condiment.

In an age when refrigeration was unknown, proper curing and storing of meat not practised, and general hygiene deplorable, our ancestors were at times compelled to eat putrid, odoriferous rations that could hardly have been delightful to look at, much less eat. Strong concoctions were perfected and served to help disguise the bad tastes. Where once these condiments were essential, they are now used to enhance and garnish any dish, especially meat and curry dishes. East Indian in origin, chutney recipes were introduced to the world by seafarers and the British who settled in India. Today chutney has universal appeal and recipes appear in culinary periodicals, cook books and newspapers. This pungent relish, made from fruit or vegetables herbs and spices, is complimentary to foods like mustard and catsup are.

In Hawaii, chutney has long been a favorite and to have jars of it stored on a shelf is to be very fortunate and rich. With our ready abundance of mangoes and all the other fresh ingredients, we are indeed able to cook up batches of this spicy sauce to last the year. But what about some of us who haven't mango trees or have missed the season? Not to worry! I have made chutney from all kinds of things. There is no end to the combinations of fruit, vegetables, spices and seasonings that yield a flavorful, rich, spicy jar of preserves. There are excellent recipes for making chutney from other than mangoes so read further in this book and see the many possibilities. One which comes the closest to tasting like mango chutney is made from canned peaches

3

and a displaced kamaaina anywhere in the world, longing for a taste of Hawaii Nei will drool with delight over this one. All preserves add color, flavor, texture and appetite appeal when included with a meal, so make up a batch of your favorite and be lavish with sharing it with others.

Read a chutney recipe thoroughly before you set about to make it and consider adjusting some of the ingredients if you feel it may be too hot, spicy, or rich. Peppers and garlic may be omitted and use less spices if you wish a milder result.

There are a few important rules to follow which will guarantee you consistently good results. Always use a stainless steel, enameled, or or agateware pan and have it large enough to afford room for the ingredients plus plenty of stirring room too. You will be greatly disappointed if you use an aluminum or iron pot as the interaction between the metals and the acids of the fruit and vinegar will impart a strange flavor and color to the preserves. Use a wooden spoon for stirring as the acidity will decompose most metal ones in time and because wood wont conduct heat to your hand or scratch the bottom of your pot. Reserve a wooden spoon just for this purpose as it will absorb flavors and taint other foods.

For best results and good consistency make chutney in small batches. When you double or triple a recipe you upset the balance and create a large amount of fruit and liquid that have a hard time thickening. If you intend to make a double portion, use two pots. Take note of the kinds of vinegar specified, it does make a difference. Use a high grade cider or white vinegar of 4–6% acidity. White has a sharper taste and is desirable when color is important, cider is more mellow and may darken fruit. Beware cider-flavor vinegar, it is simply white vinegar with caramel coloring and artificial flavoring and is not a full-bodied apple cider vinegar.

In these recipes small, red, Hawaiian chili peppers are nearly always listed, simply because they grow wild and are free, but any hot pepper will do, as well as dried pepper flakes available in jars at the market. Approach all hot peppers with extreme caution. If you have ever experienced the intolerable burning sensation that handling these peppers can produce, you know what I mean! Wear rubber gloves, or hold peppers down with a fork in one hand while you dissect and seed them with a sharp knife in the other hand. Even the fumes can cause you to cough, cry, choke and gasp for breath, so be wary when you grind them in the blender and do not inhale the steam that emits from a boiling pot. Wash your hands after touching any pepper, don't rub your eyes, and treat peppers with a profound respect for their potency!

The Hawaiian salt called for is our local rock salt and any coarse salt will serve. Young, fresh, green ginger root is always available at most local markets and especially in the Chinatown stores and at the weekly peoples open markets. Avoid the old, dried out pieces, they are tough and fibrous and cannot be grated. Pick out pieces that have a plump and shiny appearance to the skin. You can keep slivers of fresh ginger in a jar of sherry in the refrigerator. The youngest and greenest ginger root is harvested at the end of the summer months and yields the most juice and flavor and makes excellent pickles.

Preserved ginger is canned or bottled in thick syrup. Crystallized ginger is partly dried, then sugared and is readily purchased in small boxes at the market or in bulk at several shops in Chinatown. Ground ginger is the dried root which has been pulverized and is obtainable in tins or bottles at the market.

Spices in earliest times were used mainly for medicinal purposes, then it was discovered that they enhanced the flavor of bland diets and covered up the taste of food that was on the verge of spoiling. The quest for the spices of the East Indies became all-important to various countries of the world. Overland trade routes were established and fleets of ships sent out to search for spice merchants and to bring back the precious commodity.

Spices are stems, leaves, seeds, roots, bark, buds and flowers of aromatic plants grown in the tropics. Herbs are leaves and flowers of aromatic plants grown in temperate zones. Care should be taken on how you store all ground and whole spices and herbs. Forget about lining them up attractively and alphabetically right by your stove, the worst place for them! The heat, humidity and light destroy their color, taste and fragrance and you will have jars of ineffective and unsavory spices. Keep them in a cool, dark, dry place and purchase them in small amounts.

The same storage is recommended for the jars of condiments you will make. Chutney will keep well for a year or so if properly packed in sterilized jars and stored in a cool, dark, dry place. If you add nuts to your preserves, use them within six months as the nuts may turn rancid and spoil your chutney.

When a recipe says "cook to desired consistency" it is really up to you, but chutney is at its finest when the juices thicken almost to a jam stage and all the liquids are absorbed. In cooking chutney use the full cooking time specified, then test some of the liquid in a saucer, let it cool a bit, tip the saucer and see if the liquid begins to set or to run, then proceed from there.

In some Indian and Malaysian recipes the chutneys are no more than fresh ingredients and a few spices rubbed through a sieve or made with mortar and pestle, without cooking, and sometimes without enough preservative to give them more than a day's life. They are usually made daily for the main meal. In India, jars of pickles are taken outdoors into the sunshine every few days to cure them and to extend their shelflife.

A day spent making chutney or other preserves can be a long one. Plan it for a time when you don't have to cook a big meal afterward or rush off to an appointment. The preparation time is often lengthy and the cooking time usually several hours, so prepare yourself well in advance. You can begin cooking first thing in the morning if you peel and slice the mangoes the night before. Mangoes should be sliced into fairly large, thick pieces. They withstand the long cooking time and the frequent stirring, and absorb the juices better. I have often seen jars of chutney in which the mango was diced as small as frozen carrots and others where the slices were very thin. These cuts do not break down to add fiber to the liquid and usually these batches are difficult to bring to a full, thick stage. Be generous with the size of your slices and you'll have better results.

While you stir the hot, bubbly pot from time to time you can clean out kitchen drawers, wash the window over the sink, polish your nails, whatever, you're going to be around for awhile! Find a cooking parner; there are lots of cooks who are part of a chutney team and having a buddy share the tedious task is a great way to enjoy what might be a dreary activity alone. As you savor the delicious aroma that wafts up from your cooking pot, you'll know all the effort has been worth it and your neighbors will be envious.

I recall Bill Charlock's story of watching television one night at his house in Kaimuki and smelling chutney cooking, the aroma brought by the evening breeze. He went to the phone and called his aunt, Irene Zerbe Robinson who lived many streets away, and sure enough, she was making a batch of chutney and everyone for blocks around knew it.

The mango (Mangifera indica) grows and bears bountifully here in Hawaii. A native of southern Asia, the first tree was introduced here from Manila and since that date in 1824 many other varieties have been brought in from India, Jamaica, Florida and the Philippines. At one time I had a list of the hybrid strains developed from these first trees and knew where they grew in the Nuuanu area. But I've lost the information on where to find the Victoria, Sugar, Indian, Cigar, Apple, Faithful, Shibata etc. Of course the common mango, which was the original from Manila, is easily spotted because of its height and size and grows prolifically in nearly every valley and in older sections of Honolulu where there is space enough to accommodate the huge trees. Their mangoes are great for chutney but unless you have five tree-climbing young boys or a "cherry picker" you have hardly a chance to get at the glorious strands of small greenish fruit so far above the ground. (Too bad we can't get the fire department to kokua when they're not putting out fires.) The Haden, Pirie, Pope, Mapulehu and several others are cultivated in many neighborhoods and are often available in markets during the fruiting season, usually April to November.

You will find recipes that call for salting the peeled and sliced mangoes overnight and some that do not. Often it is advised to rinse the salt off before cooking, however. Some cooks say "no." some recipes call for boiling the vinegar and sugar first before adding the fruit, others do not. And there are believers in thick layers of paraffin as essential to the canning of chutney but I feel this unnecessary if your preserves are put into hot, well-sterilized jars and the cover screwed on immediately. A tight vacuum develops as the jars cool and effectively keeps the preserves. Remember to store the jars in a cool, dark, dry place.

There are chutney makers who insist that only the common mango will do, but I don't subscribe to that school of thought, especially after having peeled buckets and buckets of those teeny, hard fruit and then compared the easier task of peeling the larger Haden or Pirie which gave as good results in tasty chutney. Use whatever fruit you are fortunate enough to find and you'll have good results regardless of type.

One other tip to make canning easier. Instead of having several large, hot, steamy pots full of jars bubbling away on top of the stove, use this method to sterilize: Put your jars standing up in a large roasting pan. Fill them part way with water, pour an inch or so of water around them, lay the covers in also and place the pan on the bottom rack of a 350–375 degree oven. This leaves the stovetop clear, gives you more room to work and stir, and keeps the kitchen cooler. While your preserves cook, the jars will sterilize and be ready to receive piece de resistance. Remove them with tongs to a cloth spread on the counter and proceed with bottling and sealing the jars.

ENJOY!

The following eight mango chutney recipes are, in my estimation, among the best available. Their contributors have shared them often and they have been included in various newspaper articles and other publications.

Helen Alexander's Mango Chutney

6 pounds green mangoes, peeled and sliced
1 gallon malt vinegar
6 pounds sugar
1 pound seedless raisins
3 pounds prunes, pitted
2 pounds dates, pitted
1 pound currants
¼ pound garlic
¾ pound fresh ginger
2 pounds preserved ginger, in syrup
1 quart crushed pineapple
1 quart sliced peaches
3 teaspoons ground cinnamon
2 teaspoons ground cloves
2 teaspoons grated nutmeg
1 teaspoon cayenne pepper
1½ pounds blanched almonds
6 large green bell peppers, seeded

Sprinkle sliced mangoes with salt, let stand overnight, drain in the morning. Chop prunes, dates, preserved ginger, almonds and peppers. Skin and chop fresh ginger, cover with water and boil ½ hour. Combine sugar, vinegar, ginger syrup and spices, boil for ½ hour. Add fresh ginger and all other ingredients, except mangoes and boil slowly for 2 hours, then add mangoes and simmer for another hour, stirring constantly. Bottle while hot and seal.

Laura and Frank Bowers' Mango Chutney

20 pounds green mango slices
1 cup salt
3 quarts vinegar
1 quart water
4 large onions
12 Hawaiian red peppers, seeded
1 cup peeled and sliced gingerroot
6 to 8 cloves garlic
20 pounds white sugar
2 teaspoons cloves
2 teaspoons nutmeg
2 teaspoons allspice
2 teaspoons cinnamon
4 pounds raisins

Combine mango slices and salt and let stand overnight. Drain but do not rinse. Combine vinegar and water and heat. Put onions, peppers, ginger and garlic through a food grinder or mince finely. Add minced ingredients and mango slices to vinegar mixture and bring to a low boil. Add sugar gradually stirring after each addition. Place cloves, nutmeg, allspice and cinnamon in a spice bag or in several thicknesses of cheese cloth tied into a bag. Add bag to mango mixture. Simmer for about one hour or until mixture boils down and mango slices appear above the liquid. Add raisins, cook 5–10 minutes or until a small amount of liquid remains. Sterilize jars and fill with chutney and seal with hot paraffin then cap. Makes about 42 12 ounce jars.

Bill Garcia's Green Mango Chutney

In a blender mix the following:
½ cup chopped onion
½ cup chopped ginger root
4 or 5 red Hawaiian peppers
4 cloves garlic, chopped
the core of a fresh pineapple, finely chopped
¼ cup water
Place above in large stainless steel pot and add:
1½ cups vinegar
1½ cups water
7 cups brown sugar
1 teaspoon mustard seed
1 tablespoon salt
½ teaspoon nutmeg
½ teaspoon cloves
Boil above mixture at low heat for ½ hours and add:
1 cup currants or raisins
12 cups finely sliced green (fully developed) mangoes

Cook for about 1½ hour, low heat, stir often with wooden spoon. Mixture is done when mango slices are very tender. (Note: If mixture is dry, because of green, hard mangoes, add ½ cup water, cook additional 10 minutes.) Place the chutney in hot sterilized jars and cover with paraffin. Makes about 10 12 ounce jars.

Mango Chutney

10 pounds peeled sliced mangoes
5 pounds sugar
6 or 7 cups vinegar (depending on acidity of mangoes)
¾ cup salt
1½ pounds almonds, blanched and cut in thin strips
1 pound finely sliced candied orange peel
1 pound finely sliced candied lemon peel
2 large onions, chopped fine
2 pounds seedless raisins
1 pound finely sliced citron
⅔ cup green ginger root, cooked and chopped fine
1 cup finely chopped preserved ginger
2 cloves of garlic, chopped fine
8 small red peppers with seeds removed, chopped fine

Cut mangoes, sprinkle with salt and allow to stand overnight.* Boil the sugar and vinegar 5 minutes. Add to the drained mango pulp, cook until tender; then add the other ingredients and cook slowly for ½ to 1 hour or until the desired consistency is obtained. Pour into hot sterile *jars* and seal immediately. Serve with meat or curried dishes.
* do not wash salt off, just drain

Bulletin No. 77
Hawaii Agriculture Experiment Station
Also Called Punahou School Mango Chutney

Hawaiian Electric's Mango Chutney

12 cups sliced green mangoes
8 tablespoons salt
7 cups (3 pounds) raw sugar
3 cups vinegar
2 15 oz. packages raisins
4 Hawaiian red peppers, chopped
3 tablespoons finely chopped garlic
½ cup finely chopped ginger root
3 cups slivered almonds

Combine mango slices and salt and let stand overnight. Rinse with cold water and drain. Combine sugar and vinegar and simmer for ½ hour. Add mango slices and remaining ingredients; simmer for 1 hour or until mangoes are tender and chutney is of desired consistency. Pour into sterilized jars and seal.

May Moir's Mango Chutney

7½ pounds sliced green mangoes
7½ pounds dark brown sugar
1½ quarts cider vinegar
1 package raisins, whole
1 package raisins, chopped or ground
½ package currants, whole
1 thumb-sized piece of ginger root, chopped
12 red chili peppers (small Hawaiian type, whole)
1 clove garlic, chopped (optional)

Simmer all ingredients except the mango slices for half an hour. After sauce is well blended, bring to boil and add the mango slices. Continue to boil until the fruit looks translucent. Turn off the heat, cover the pot with a clean dishcloth and let stand for half a day or overnight. Next day reheat the chutney to a boil and when thickened pour into hot, sterilized jars and seal.

Vivian Shinmoto's Mango Chutney

10 cups diced or sliced mangoes, preferably the Chinese or common ones
2 handfuls Hawaiian salt
3½ cups white sugar
3½ cups brown sugar
¾ cup raisins
1 cup onions chopped
¾ cup currrants
½ cup ginger root, chopped
5 cloves garlic, minced
7 chili peppers, chopped fine
2 cups vinegar
1 cup water
½ cup blanched and slivered almonds

Sprinkle Hawaiian salt over mangoes and let stand overnight. Boil the rest of the ingredients for about 15 minutes. Add drained mangoes and cook slowly for about 1½ hours. About 10 minutes before removing from heat, add ½ teaspoon cinnamon, ½ teaspoon nutmeg, ½ teaspoon allspice and ¼ teaspoon cloves. Pour into sterilized jars and seal.

Oven Method Mango Chutney

Any of the simpler chutney recipes can be made this way instead of by the stove top method. After all ingredients are assembled, put them in a large enameled roasting pan and cook uncovered in a 375 degree oven, stirring often, for 3 to 3½ hours. Check to see that liquid has not been cooked away; add small amount of water if it has and continue to stir until desired consistency has been attained. Bottle and seal.

The next three mango chutney recipes are from a collection dating back to the days of the Hawaiian monarchy.

Mrs. Bishop's Chutney

9 pounds mangoes
4 pounds dark brown sugar
1 pound raisins, seeded
1 pound currants
1 pound almonds, chopped
6 cups dark vinegar
2 tablespoons coarse Hawaiian salt
2 tablespoons chopped green ginger
½ tablespoon garlic, chopped fine
Chili pepper or Tabasco to taste

Peel mangoes. Cut into large slices. Boil mango slices in vinegar for 1 hour. Add the remaining ingredients and boil about 1 hour longer, or until thick. Cool. Pour into sterilized jars.

Mrs. Guillaume's Mango Chutney

½ cup Hawaiian salt
6 onions
1 quart vinegar
2 tablespoons ginger root, ground in food chopper
3 tablespoons garlic, ground as above
½ pound raisins
½ pound currants
1 teaspoon ground cloves
1 teaspoon ground cinnamon
½ teaspoon ground nutmeg
1 pound chopped almonds
¼ pound chopped citron
1 dozen small red peppers
8 pounds mangoes
8 pounds sugar

Slice mangoes and sprinkle with salt. Let stand overnight. Pour off juice. To the juice, add ground onions, ginger and garlic. Add spices and vinegar and cook until tender. Add the mangoes and sugar. In the meantime boil red peppers in a cloth bag in water for 1 hour. Add these with remainder of ingredients to the mango mixture and cook for 2 hours. Let stand overnight. Boil 2 more hours. Add about 3 diced mangoes and cook 15 minutes (if you want to have some whole chunks in your chutney). Otherwise this step isn't necessary. Bottle and seal.

Mrs. Lansing's Chutney

25 pounds mangoes
15 pounds brown sugar
¼ pound ground green ginger
¼ pound ground garlic
1 quart dark vinegar
12 large hot peppers or 18 small ones
2 pounds seedless raisins
2½ pounds currants
1 cup preserved mixed candied fruit (orange, citron and lemon)
3 large onions
1½ pounds pitted dates
1 tablespoon nutmeg
1 tablespoon cloves
1 tablespoon cinnamon
1 tablespoon allspice

Peel mangoes. Cut into large slices. Cover with 2 handfuls coarse salt. Let stand overnight. Drain the next morning. Cut up the candied fruit. Coarsely chop onions. Cut dates in halves. Put peppers into cheesecloth bag. Cook together over medium heat for 15 minutes all ingredients except the mangoes. Then add the mangoes, and stirring frequently, cook until mangoes are clear but hold their shape. Cool. Spoon into sterilized jars.

Sofer Chutney

8 pounds mangoes, peeled and sliced
8 pounds brown sugar
2 medium onions, chopped
1 pound raisins, seedless
2 tablespoons green ginger, grated
pinch of cayenne
16 cloves
3 tablespoons salt
2 cloves garlic, chopped
1 cup vinegar
coarse salt
small red Hawaiian pepper

Sprinkle mango slices with a handful of salt and leave to soak overnight. Drain mangoes the next morning. Plump raisins in sherry. Put small red Hawaiian peppers (4 to 18 depending on how hot you like your chutney) into a little cheesecloth bag. Mix together all ingredients except the mangoes. Cook for 15 minutes over medium heat. Add mangoes, stirring frequently and cook until mangoes appear clear. Cool. Pour into sterilized jars.

The remainder of the chutney recipes all use various fruit as the main ingredient as opposed to the typical mango we are accustomed to.

Mixed Fruit Chutney

1 cup seedless prunes, chopped
1 cup seedless dark raisins
2 cups tart green apples, peeled, cored and chopped
1 cup ripe tomatoes peeled and chopped
1 cup onions, chopped
1½ cups cider vinegar
2 cups light brown sugar
2 cloves garlic, minced
2 small hot, red peppers, seeded and chopped
1 tablespoon grated lemon peel
1 teaspoon salt
1 teaspoon ground cinnamon

In a pan put vinegar, sugar, cinnamon, salt, garlic and peppers and bring to a boil; add all other ingredients. Reduce heat, cover, and continue to cook, stirring often until mixture is desired consistency, about 30 to 45 minutes. Pour into hot, sterilized jars and seal.

Fig Chutney

2½ cups diced, ripe figs
½ cup raisins
¼ cup chopped crystallized ginger
1 cup brown sugar
1 cup cider vinegar
½ lemon, peeled, seeded, chopped fine
1 clove garlic, minced
1 scant teaspoon salt
pinch cayenne
spice bundle, in cheesecloth – 6 cloves, 6 allspice berries,
    1 stick cinnamon, pinch nutmeg
1 tablespoon chili powder

Bring sugar and vinegar to a boil, add all ingredients, return to a boil, reduce heat and stir often. Continue cooking until mixture becomes very thick, approximately 1¼ to 2 hours. Discard spices, pour into hot, sterilized jars, let cool. Refrigerate and let mellow several days before serving. (Cook over very low heat and watch to see mixture does not scorch.)

Apricot Date Chutney
Using dried fruit

2 cups dried apricots, chopped
1 cup dates, pitted and chopped
1 cup brown sugar
1 cup white sugar
1 cup cider vinegar
1 small onion, chopped
1½ tablespoons grated fresh ginger root
3–4 red Hawaiian chili peppers (optional)
juice of 1 lime
2 garlic cloves, chopped
1¼ cups water

Placed dried fruit in a bowl and pour boiling water over to cover. Let stand several hours or overnight. Combine vinegar, sugars and all other ingredients, bring to boiling, reduce heat and simmer uncovered about 20–30 minutes, until mixture begins to thicken. Stir *drained* apricots and dates into pot and continue cooking another 20–30 minutes until it has reached the desired consistency. Pour into hot, sterilized jars and seal.

Hot and Spicy Citrus Chutney

½ pound kumquats or Calamondin fruit
½ cup honey
3 cups cider vinegar
½ pound rhubarb, chopped fine
1 cup celery, diced
½ cup water
2½ cups dark brown sugar
1 large onion, minced
1 green pepper, chopped
2 cloves garlic, crushed
1 cup raisins
¼ cup chopped citron
grated rind and juice of 1 orange
1 teaspoon each ground cinnamon, allspice, ginger, curry powder
2 teaspoons salt
1 tablespoon Worcestershire sauce

Slice kumquats, remove seeds, combine with honey and cook over medium heat for 30 minutes. Add remaining ingredients and simmer 1 hour or until mixture thickens. Pour into hot sterlized jars and seal.

Papaya Chutney

3–4 papayas, pared, seeded, and cut into small chunks
1 8–oz. can crushed pineapple, drained
1¼ cups cider vinegar
1¼ cups brown sugar
1 tablespoon rock salt
½ teaspoon allspice
½ teaspoon cloves
¾ cup golden raisins
1 tablespoon seeded and crushed Hawaiian chili pepper
1 tablespoon grated fresh green ginger root

In large saucepan place the vinegar, sugar, and salt and bring to a boil, then lower heat and cook over medium heat for 3 minutes. Add the papaya chunks, pineapple, raisins, ginger and spices and return to a boil and continue cooking and stirring until fruit is tender and desired consistency has been reached, about 10 minutes. Pack into hot sterilized jars and seal.

Cranberry Chutney

4 cups fresh or frozen cranberries
1½ cups brown sugar
½ cup orange juice concentrate
½ cup cider vinegar
¼ cup water
¾ cup chopped onion
½ cup minced celery
1 medium green apple, peeled, cored and chopped
1 teaspoon ground cloves
1 teaspoon ground allspice
1 teaspoon ground cinnamon
½ teaspoon cayenne pepper

In a pan, combine berries, raisins, orange juice concentrate, sugar, water, vinegar and cook over medium heat until berries start to pop, about 10 minutes. Stir in spices, onion, celery and apple; simmer uncovered about 45 minutes until most of liquid is absorbed, stirring frequently. If hotter chutney is desired, add chopped and seeded red Hawaiian peppers, about 4 of them. When right consistency, bottle and seal. Buy bags of cranberries during the Thanksgiving and Christmas holidays and keep them in freezer for later use.

Tomato Chutney

1 cup white vinegar
1 thumbsized piece ginger root
4 cloves garlic
4 pounds ripe tomatoes, peeled, seeded, and chopped
1 cup brown sugar
1 teaspoon salt
2 small hot red peppers (seeded and minced) or ½ teaspoon cayenne
½ cup golden raisins
¼ cup blanched slivered almonds
1 teaspoon grated lemon peel

In a blender combine the ginger and garlic with ½ cup of the vinegar and blend just until they are minced, then put the mixture in large pan with tomatoes, remaining vinegar and sugar, salt, peppers, and bring to a boil. Reduce heat and simmer, uncovered, stirring frequently until nearly all liquid is absorbed, about 2 hours. Stir in raisins, lemon peel and almonds and cook just a few minutes more. Pour into hot sterilized jars and seal.

Pineapple Chutney

2 ounces small red peppers with seeds removed, chopped fine
1 ounce or 1 medium-sized bulb of garlic, chopped fine
2 tablespoons of finely chopped fresh ginger root
1 tablespoon salt
3 pounds peeled pineapple
1½ pounds brown sugar
1½ pints vinegar
½ pound seedless raisins
½ pound blanched almonds, chopped fine

Cut the pineapple in small pieces, add vinegar and salt, cook slowly until pineapple is tender. Add the other ingredients and boil slowly until desired consistency is obtained. Pour into hot sterile jars and seal immediately.

Bulletin 77
Hawaii Experiment Station
3rd printing January 1939

Date Chutney

3 cups pitted dates, coarsely chopped (about 1 pound)
1 cup cider vinegar
1 cup water
1½ tablespoons mustard seed
½ teaspoon black pepper
½ teaspoon dried hot red pepper flakes
¼ teaspoon allspice
¼ teaspoon ground cloves

In a large pan combine dates with all other ingredients, cook over medium high heat, mashing dates with a heavy spoon and stirring the mixture until it begins to thicken, about 10 minutes. When it has reached desired consistency, pour into hot sterilized jars and seal.

Nectarine Chutney

1 pound pitted fresh nectarines, chopped
1 small red bell pepper, seeded and chopped
2 medium onions, coarsely chopped
2 lemons, seeded but not peeled, finely chopped
1 tablespoon fresh young ginger root, grated
3 tablespoons crystallized ginger, minced
2½ cups brown sugar
½ cup cider vinegar
½ teaspoon salt
2 hot red peppers, seeded and minced, or
    ½ teaspoon cayenne pepper
½ teaspoon ground allspice

In large pan bring to boiling the sugar, vinegar, salt, peppers, ginger and allspice, reduce heat and simmer 10–15 minutes. Add all remaining ingredients, bring back to boiling, reduce heat and simmer, stirring frequently, until thickened, 30–45 minutes. Pour into hot, sterilized jars and seal.

Rhubarb Chutney

2 pounds fresh rhubarb, cleaned and cut into 1-inch pieces or
    2 16 ounce bags of frozen rhubarb, thawed
2 cups light brown sugar
1 cup chopped onion
1 cup cider vinegar
¼ cup currants
¼ cup golden raisins
1 tablespoon curry powder
1 tablespoon grated fresh ginger root
1 clove garlic, chopped
1 teaspoon salt

Combine all ingredients in pan, heat over medium heat to boiling, stir often. Reduce heat, cook uncovered until mixture thickens, about one hour, stirring frequently. Pour into hot sterilized jars and seal.

Kiwifruit Chutney

3 medium apples (about 1 pound)
1 clove garlic, finely chopped
2 tablespoons lime juice
1 cup light brown sugar
1 cup cider vinegar
1 cup golden raisins
¼ teaspoon salt
½ teaspoon ground cinnamon
½ teaspoon ground ginger or fresh grated ginger root
½ teaspoon ground cumin
6 kiwifruit

Peel, core and cut apples into ½-inch cubes (about 3½ cups). Put cut up apples with all other ingredients, *except* kiwifruit, stir together and boil gently, stirring often, for 20 minutes. Peel and cut kiwifruit into small cubes, add to the pot. Bring to boil again and simmer gently, stirring, until thickened, another 20 minutes. Seal in hot, sterilized jars.

Tomato and Apple Chutney

6 pounds green tomatoes
4 pounds tart green apples
3 large onions
1½ pounds brown sugar
½ can mustard seed (about 1 ounce)
2 teaspoons cayenne pepper
2 tablespoons salt
4 cups white vinegar

Peel but do not seed tomatoes, then coarsely chop. Peel, core, and chop apples and also chop onions coarsely. Put all ingredients in a large pan, bring to a boil, reduce heat, simmer, covered, 2 to 2½-hours, checking liquid level. When right consistency, pour into hot sterilized jars and seal.

Tomato-Pear Chutney

2½ cups tomatoes, quartered (fresh or canned)
2½ cups Bartlett pears, diced (fresh or canned)
½ cup golden raisins
½ cup green bell pepper, chopped
½ cup onion, chopped
½ cup white vinegar
1 teaspoon salt
½ teaspoon ground ginger
½ teaspoon powdered dry mustard
1/8 teaspoon cayenne pepper
¼ cup canned pimiento, chopped

Peel the tomatoes and pears and combine all ingredients, including the juice of the can of pears only, in a pan, with exception of pimiento. Bring to a boil, reduce heat and cook slowly, about 45 minutes, stirring often. Then add pimiento and boil 3 minutes until desired consistency is reached. Pack into hot, sterilized jars and seal.

U.S. Department of Agriculture bulletin

Fresh Indian Chutneys

These are several kinds of Indian chutney which are made fresh daily, without preservatives and intended for immediate use, or will keep a few days under refrigeration.

MINT   1 cup chopped mint leaves, ½ cup chopped green onions, 1 tablespoon finely chopped fresh ginger, 2 hot green chili peppers, ½ teaspoon salt and juice of 1 lemon. Place mint, ginger, onions and peppers in electric blender jar. Add salt and squeeze lemon over all and blend to a fine paste. (Beware of pepper fumes when removing cover) This is a strong, hot chutney and good with lamb and chicken.

RAISIN 1 cup raisins, 1 tablespoon freshly grated ginger, ½ teaspoon cayenne pepper, ½ teaspoon salt, 4 tablespoons water, juice of half a lemon. Place all ingredients in blender, in same order as above and blend to a fine paste. This is milder chutney and tasty with pork, ham, and chicken.

COCONUT 1 cup grated fresh coconut, ½ cup water, 3 tablespoons tamarind pulp* or juice of 1 lemon, 1 tablespoon brown sugar, 2 hot green chili peppers, 1 tablespoon grated fresh ginger, ½ teaspoon salt, and 1 cup coriander leaves (Chinese parsley) Follow same method as above. Excellent with nearly all meats.

*Tamarind notes on page 35

Tamarind Chutney

Indian Recipe

One-half pound tamarinds, ½ pound dates, ½ pound green ginger, ½ pound raisins, ½ pound onions, ¼ pound chilis, 4 tablespoonfuls brown sugar, 2 tablespoonfuls salt. Pound all with vinegar and rub through a sieve. Bottle and cork.

This rather sketchy recipe is from the Womans' Society of Central Union cookbook and although sounds like a lot of work, it does have possibilities for a tasty, no-cook, no-chunk version of chutney.

Tamarind trees of the Senna family (Tamarindus indica L.) are common to Hawaii and a native of Asia and tropical Africa. Their pods yield a sticky, thick pulp which has been used in making drinks, chutneys and curries. Large trees grow in many places on Oahu as well as the outside islands, and their pods can be picked up from the ground, steeped to make tamarind ade, dried in the sun much like litchi, preserved in sugar, or dried and compressed into a hard slab which can be bought in Chinatown. Pieces of it soaked in water will render an instant pulp.

Peach Chutney
using canned peaches

4 9½ oz. cans peach halves or sliced peaches
2 cups brown sugar
2 cups white vinegar
2 cloves garlic, minced
⅓ cup red bell pepper, diced
¼ cup crystallized ginger, minced
¼ cup fresh green ginger root, grated
2 small hot red peppers, seeded and minced
1 teaspoon salt
1 teaspoon ground cinnamon
1 tablespoon whole cloves
1 cup golden raisins

Drain peaches,, reserve syrup, cut halves into small pieces. In large pan combine syrup with all other ingredients, except peaches, bring to boiling and boil rapidly, uncovered, about 30 minutes, stirring occasionally. Stir in peaches, continue to boil gently until mixture is thickened, about 30 to 45 minutes. When desired consistency has been reached, pour into hot, sterilized jars and seal.

Pear and Ginger Chutney

5 pounds firm but ripe Bartlett pears, peeled, cored, and cubed
1 large onion, coarsely chopped
1 cup fresh green ginger root, peeled and thinly slivered
2 cloves garlic, minced
1 lemon, thinly sliced, seeded but not peeled
1½ cups cider vinegar
1½ cups brown sugar
½ cup currants
½ teaspoon ground allspice

In a large pan combine all ingredients, bring to a boil, reduce heat, simmer uncovered, stirring frequently, until juices have been absorbed and desired consistency has been attained, about 1½ hours.

Citrus Chutney

4 large oranges
1¾ cup brown sugar
¾ cup chopped onion
¾ cup raisins
¼ cup lemon juice
¼ cup lime juice
2 tablespoons grated fresh ginger root
1 teaspoon salt
2 cloves garlic, chopped
½ teaspoon ground cinnamon
½ teaspoon ground cloves
½ teaspoon ground allspice
½ cup chopped almonds or walnuts

Peel oranges, chop enough rind to make ⅓ cup finely chopped peel. Section fruit over bowl to reserve juice, discard membranes. In pan place fruit and peel, sugar, and remainder of ingredients, except nuts. Bring to boil, then add nuts, reduce heat and keep at gentle boil, uncovered, for 30 minutes or until mixture thickens, stirring frequently. Cool, then place in sterilized jars.

Indian Apple Chutney

6 pounds tart green apples, not peeled, cut into chunks
3 pounds dark brown sugar
3 pounds dark seedless raisins
3 pounds pitted dates, cut into pieces
¾ pound preserved ginger – see below
6 cups spiced cider vinegar – see below
3 medium onions, chopped
6 cloves garlic, minced
6 hot red peppers, seeded and chopped
2 tablespoons salt

In a pan bring vinegar, apples, onion and garlic and peppers to a boil, reduce heat and cook until apples are tender. Add all other ingredients and bring back to a full boil, reduce heat and simmer, uncovered and stirring frequently, until mixture begins to thicken and desired consistency has been reached, about 45 minutes. Pour into hot, sterilized jars and seal.

To preserve ginger: boil root in water for ½ hour, drain, and chop. Spiced vinegar: In a piece of cheesecloth put 4 sticks of cinnamon, 1 tablespoon whole cloves and 1 tablespoon whole allspice and tie up. Place bundle in pan with 2 quarts vinegar and boil for 15 minutes.

Apple Orange Peel Chutney

8 cups tart green apples, peeled, cored and chopped
4 cups brown sugar
1 cup dark raisins
1 cup golden raisins
peel of 2 oranges, finely minced
1 cup walnuts, chopped
2 cloves garlic, finely minced
½ cup cider vinegar
½ teaspoon cloves

In large pan place all ingredients and bring to a boil, stirring frequently. Reduce heat, simmer until apples are soft and syrup has thickened and desired consistency has been attained, about 1 hour. Pour into hot, sterilized jars and seal.

Apple and Bell Pepper Chutney

7 cups tart green apples, pared, cored, coarsely chopped
7 cups firm ripe tomatoes, coarsely chopped
3 cups onions, coarsely chopped
1½ cups red bell pepper, coarsely chopped
1½ cups green bell pepper, coarsely chopped
¾ cup dark raisins
¾ cup golden raisins
½ cup sliced celery, strings removed
⅓ cup crystallized ginger, chopped
4 cups cider vinegar
1½ cups brown sugar
1 tablespoon salt

In a large pan bring vinegar, sugar and salt to the boil, add all remaining ingredients, reduce heat and simmer, stirring frequently, until chutney has thickened to desired consistency, about 1½ hours. Pour into hot sterilized jars and seal.

Beetroot Chutney

1 pound apples, peeled, cored and chopped
3 pounds cooked beets, chopped small
1 pound onions, chopped
3 cloves garlic, chopped
½ cup raisins
2 cups white vinegar
2¼ cups white sugar
2 teaspoons salt
8 whole cloves

Cook the onions for a short while in a little of the vinegar. Add the rest of the ingredients. Cook gently, stirring to avoid sticking. When soft add the rest of the vinegar and sugar and cook slowly for about 30 minutes. Pour into hot, sterilized jars and seal.

Watermelon Rind Chutney

4 cups prepared watermelon rind, red meat removed,
    green skin removed
2 tablespoons salt
1¼ cup white sugar
1¼ cups cider vinegar
1¼ cups light corn syrup
½ lemon, peeled, seeded, and sliced (white membrane removed)
½ cup golden raisins
¼ cup chopped onion
2 small cloves garlic, minced
½ teaspoon powdered ginger or
    1 tablespoon grated fresh ginger root
¼ teaspoon ground cinnamon

Cut white rind portion of watermelon into ½-inch cubes, cover with water in a bowl, add the salt, let stand 2 hours. Drain, rinse under cold running water, drain again in colander. In large pan place rind and just barely cover with cold water, bring to a boil and boil gently until tender but not soft, about 30 minutes. Drain. In another pan mix all other ingredients, add rind, bring to boil, reduce heat and simmer, uncovered, until rind is transparent and syrup has begun to thicken, about 1½ hours. When desired consistency has been reached, pour into hot, sterilized jars and seal.

Melon Chutney

2 firm medium cantaloupes, seeded, pared and cubed
    into ½ inch pieces
1 firm medium honeydew, seeded, pared and cubed into
    ½ inch pieces
2 medium onions, coarsely chopped
2 green bell peppers, coarsely chopped
4 cups brown sugar
3½ cups white vinegar
⅓ cup crystallized ginger, finely chopped
2 cloves garlic, finely chopped
1 large lime, seeded and thinly siced, with peel
1 tablespoon ground cinnamon
2 teaspoons salt
1 teaspoon ground cloves
1 teaspoon ground allspice

Put all ingredients in a large pan, bring to a boil, reduce heat and simmer, uncovered, stirring frequently, for 1½ to 2 hours, until the mixture begins to thicken. When of the desired consistency, pour into hot sterilized jars and seal.

Apple and Citrus Chutney

6 cups of green apples, unpeeled and chopped
2 limes, chopped
2 lemons, chopped
2 green tomatoes, chopped
2 large onions, chopped
1 cup golden raisins
4 cloves garlic, chopped
2 cups cider vinegar
1½ cups white sugar
4 teaspoons fresh green ginger root, minced
2 teaspoons salt
1 teaspoon dried red pepper flakes

Combine all ingredients in a large pan and cook uncovered over moderate heat, stirring often, for 1–1½ hours or until the mixture thickens. Pour into hot, sterilized jars, seal immediately, store in a cool, dark place to cure, about 1–2 weeks before serving.

Apple and Tomato Chutney

5 cups of peeled and chopped cooking apples
1 15-ounce can (2 cups) tomato sauce
2 cups brown sugar
1½ cups golden raisins
¾ cup vinegar
½ cup chopped onion
½ cup lemon juice
1 tablespoons grated fresh ginger root
3 cloves garlic, chopped
3 red Hawaiian peppers, seeded and chopped
1 teaspoon salt

In large pan combine all ingredients, bring mixture to boiling, stirring to dissolve sugar. Reduce heat and boil gently, uncovered, for 40–50 minutes or until it thickens, stirring often. Pour into hot sterilized jars and seal.

Now for my favorite chutney story. I went to visit Charlie Robinson one day and his Nuuanu kitchen was hot and steamy with the acrid smell of vinegar. I choked my way through the door, past counter after counter laden with sticky, dark jars of pungent mango chutney and, tears streaming down my face and my hair falling limp, I talked chutney with him. Charlie liked to cook and had been busy for days, peeling, slicing, and cooking mangoes and had already bottled upwards of a hundred jars. I picked up one near me, held it to the light like all cooks do, and watched the contents slosh about as I tipped it. I said, "Uh, Charlie, this batch doesn't seem to have cooked long enough," and he replied in his wonderful, droll way, "I know, but I'm using Christian Science on it; in divine mind there's no such thing as runny chutney" and went right on with his cooking and stirring.

CURRY

Curry

Volumes have been written about curry and its origins. Some say "from the Hindi *turcarri,* meaning sauce, comes the English word curry", while another view is, "the word 'curry' is said to derive from the *Tamil keri,* but experts seem to disagree on the meaning. Some say *keri* means marketplace or bazaar, others claim it stands for anything made with yoghurt." Surely the British in India can be credited with the origin of modern curry, but while curries are based on traditional Indian cookery, they may well have been invented by Europeans. Another observer said "there has probably been more flap about curries than any other form of cooking in the whole world."

Regardless of the pros and cons one thing that curry lovers agree on is the supreme delight attained in feasting on a colorful, spicy, tasty curry supper complete with the chutneys and sambals, or side dishes, traditionally served with curry. Curry suppers have long been a part of Island entertaining and a favorite form of presenting hospitality, especially to visitors to Hawaii.

This next section is devoted to the preparation of curry powders, the sauces which flavor and accompany the main dish, the rice served with the dishes, and the variety of condiments, beverages, and light desserts which are part of a curry supper.

Curries differ from country to country; Thai curries are heavily seasoned with chili peppers and are the hottest of their kind. Vindaloo curries from the south of India contain vinegar and mustard oil as a preservative in the hot climate. Yoghurt is usually included in the Koorma curries typical of northern India. Coconut milk or cream is almost always a part of the curries of Sri Lanka and the curries of the West Indies are heavy with a combination of peppers and fragrant spices.

There are a few rules to follow in curry-making and the most important is to use only clarified butter in preparing the sauce as it doesn't burn or spatter as solid butter, margarine or oil will. In India this is called *ghee* and you'll find the recipe in this section.

Ingredients such as onion, peppers, garlic and gingerroot should be chopped very fine and the spices, or curry powder, should be lightly fried in *ghee* for several minutes to elimimate the raw taste, or toasted first in a hot oven. Never thicken the sauce with cornstarch or flour, it will create an inferior sauce as well as stick to the bottom of the pan. To thicken, remove lid from pan and let sauce thicken by reduction.

To add acidity to some curries, use limes, lemons, a bit of vinegar, or tamarinds, instead of salting heavily. Yoghurt, fresh or sour milk can be used when coconut milk is not available.

Now a word about the spices used to flavor a curry sauce. In India the combination of the spices is called *garam masala* whereas the English version is called curry powder. *Garam masala* whose name means 'the warming spices' is added near the end of the cooking of a dish to give it life, while curry powders containing the hot spices such as chili are used throughout the cooking process. *Garam masala* may have been the inspiration for curry powder and there are cooks who favor one over the other. Make powdered spices in small batches as they lose their potency in a month or so, (which may be one good reason why some curries just don't have the right "zip" they should). Store them in airtight glass jars with tight lids and place them in a cool, dry, dark place. There is a big difference between these spice combinations and the commercial variety purchased at the market. Freshly ground spices are more flavorful and impart a more authentic taste to curry dishes. Experiment with the recipes that follow and make adjustments to your liking.

A Simple Curry Powder No. 1

½ cup coriander seeds
2 tablespoons saffron threads
1 tablespoon cumin seeds
1 tablespoon mustard seeds
1½ teaspoons crushed red pepper
1 tablespoon poppy seeds

Grind the above in a peppermill or coffeegrinder and store in an airtight jar in a cool, dark, dry place.

A Hotter Version No. 2

½ cup coriander seeds
½ cup turmeric, ground
4 tablespoons black peppercorns
1 tablespoon red pepper flakes
1 tablespoon ginger
1 tablespoon cumin seeds
½ teaspoon cayenne pepper

Grind the above in a peppermill or coffeegrinder and store in an airtight jar in a cool, dark, dry place.

Hot Curry Powder
From Ground Spices No. 3

Pinch of fenugreek*
2 tablespoons ground turmeric
4 teaspoons ground coriander
4 teaspoons cayenne pepper
2 teaspoons dry mustard
2 teaspoons ground cumin
2 teaspoons ground cardamom
2 teaspoons ground cinnamon
2 teaspoons ground ginger
1 teaspoon ground cloves
1 teaspoon ground black pepper

Whirl all ingredients in coffeegrinder or blender and store in tightly covered glass jar in dark, cool, dry place.

*An Asiatic herb with aromatic seeds used in making curry.

Garam Masala
Indian Spice

3 tablespoons whole black peppercorns
2 tablespoons cumin seeds
2 tablespoons coriander seeds
1 3-inch stick cinnamon, crushed
2 tablespoons whole cloves
8 cardamoms, seeds removed
6 bay leaves, crushed

Roast the spices in a heavy iron skillet over high heat to toast them, stirring constantly to prevent burning them. When cool, whirl in electric grinder or spice mill and store in glass jar with tight lid in a cool, dark, dry place. Use this spice in Indian cooking or to season vegetables or chicken.

Note: toast the cumin and coriander separately, they should not be heated in the same pan. The spices' aroma may linger in the grinder, so clean well after use or reserve one just for the purpose. If spices have not all ground to a uniform powder you may want to sieve them before placing in the jar.

West Indian Curry Powder

¼ cup coriander seeds
¼ cup black peppercorns
½ cup white cumin seeds
1 tablespoon cloves
1 tablespoon poppy seeds
1 tablespoon brown mustard seeds
4 tablespoons ground Jamaican ginger
½ cup ground turmeric

Mix all seeds in a heavy skillet and dry roast the spices, stirring, over low heat until they begin to pop and emit their aroma. Remove from pan and grind in a blender to a fine powder. Sieve and keep grinding, add turmeric and swirl all together again. Store in air tight jar up to a month.

Curry Paste No. 1

6 tablespoons coriander
1 heaped teaspoon anise seed
1 heaped teaspoon allspice
1 heaped teaspoon turmeric or saffron
1 heaped teaspoon cardamom
1 heaped teaspoon cinnamon
1 heaped teaspoon black peppercorns
1 teaspoon mustard seed
3 cloves garlic, crushed
1 large onion, chopped
red pepper to taste

Grind on a stone, in a mortar, or in a blender. Grind turmeric first and add enough water to make a stiff paste. Gradually add other ingredients, grinding slowly to a fine consistency. If not being used that day, omit onion, garlic and red pepper. Store the paste in a tightly covered jar in refrigerator and add garlic, onion and red pepper before using. Makes a really hot curry!

Curry Paste No. 2

2 teaspoons coriander
1 teaspoon turmeric
½ teaspoon cumin
½ teaspoon ginger
½ teaspoon cinnamon
½ teaspoon cardamom
½ teaspoon chilies (red pepper flakes)
¼ teaspoon cracked black peppercorns

Grind the above in an electric peppermill then blend in a heavy pan over low heat with 2 tablespoons clarified butter (see *ghee*). Stirring constantly, cook the spices about 5 minutes, cool and store in airtight jar in the refrigerator.

Ghee

Clarified Butter

Put a half-pound or more of unsalted butter in a pan over moderate heat and let it melt slowly. Water will evaporate, leaving sediment at the bottom, the milk solids. Scum will rise to the surface and should be removed. When the butter is clear, ladle the clarified liquid into a sieve lined with muslin or cheesecloth and store the *ghee* in a covered container, under refrigeration, for up to 3 months. Discard the sediment.

Tamarind Juice

Native to tropical Africa and southern Asia, the tamarind (Tamarindus indica) was first planted in Honolulu by Don Marin in Pauoa Valley in 1797, and on the grounds of the Catholic cathedral on upper Fort Street. This rough-barked tree can attain a height of 40–50 feet in Hawaii and has feathery, graceful branches which cascade down bearing the thick, velvety pods containing a sticky, brown pulp. As the pods mature, the outer shell becomes hard and brittle and the pulp pulls away from the shell and is easily extracted. The pulp has an unusually high acid and sugar content and is high in calcium and phosphorus. The pulp has been popular in Hawaii for making tamarindade, a refreshing drink. In the tree's native countries the pods are as popular as dried figs and dates.

Two methods of preserving the shelled and seeded pods are to press the pulp into cakes and store them under refrigeration or to pack the whole pods in jars of sugar to keep them. The pulp can be pureed and cooked and thinned with water for later use as a substitute for lemons or limes. Tamarind juice is an essential ingredient of curries and chutneys and in the Orient it is used to pickle fish.

To extract juice from fresh pods, steep them in water to cover, let stand overnight and drain through a sieve the next day, pressing pulp through along with the water. Place mixture in a sterilized jar and refrigerate. Dried slabs of compressed tamarind pulp can also be found in Asian markets in Chinatown.

Simple Chicken Curry

8 small chicken pieces, skinned
4 medium onions, chopped
1 piece fresh ginger root, finely minced
2 cloves garlic, finely minced
1 teaspoon turmeric
1 teaspoon chili powder
2 teaspoons ground coriander
1 teaspoon garam masala (see garam masala)
salt to taste
4 tablespoons yoghurt
1 tablespoon clarified butter (see ghee)

Grind onions, ginger and garlic to smooth paste. Heat ghee in pan, add paste and fry it, stirring frequently, to a rich golden color. Add a little water to prevent sticking. Sprinkle spices and salt into the pan, stir well and continue cooking a few minutes. Lightly whip yoghurt and add it a little at a time, stirring continuously and cook until most of the moisture has evaporated and the mixture is rich and brown. Add chicken pieces and brown, turning frequently until golden. Pour a little water over the pan, stir well, cover pan and cook until chicken is tender and sauce has thickened, about 1 hour.

A Basic Curry Sauce for
Chicken, Lamb, Shrimp. Etc.

2 cups of chicken stock
1 onion, finely minced
1 green apple, finely chopped
1 clove garlic, crushed
1 teaspoon finely minced fresh ginger root
2 tablespoons curry powder (see curry powder)
3 tablespoons clarified butter (see *ghee*)
1 cup coconut milk (see coconut milk)
1 tablespoon lemon juice

Saute onion, garlic and ginger in oil, add curry powder and cook until lightly browned. Add green apple which will help thicken sauce and cook 5 minutes. Add stock and cook 20 minutes, stirring occasionally, until thickened. Put into sauce up to 3 cups of cooked meat or shellfish, then add coconut milk to desired consistency, stirring well. If the sauce is too bland add lemon juice to taste.

Murgi Bade Sabha
Chicken with almonds in spicy sauce
Northern India

2½# chicken, skinned and cut into 8 pieces
1 round onion, chopped
1 piece fresh ginger root, chopped
1 green chili, seeded and chopped
2 cloves garlic, crushed
1 teaspoon ground cumin
2 bay leaves
6 whole cloves
4 green cardamoms
6 black peppercorns
2 1-inch pieces stick cinnamon
2 teaspoons ground fennel seeds
1 teaspoon chili powder
½ teaspoon turmeric
1 teaspoon dried mint or 2 teaspoons fresh mint, chopped
salt to taste
3 tablespoons yoghurt
½ pound ripe tomatoes, chopped
6 tablespoons clarified butter (see *ghee*)
1 tablespoons chopped coriander (Chinese parsley)
½ cup slivered, lightly toasted almonds

Mix onions, ginger, chili and garlic together and spoon a layer of this into bottom of heavy saucepan. Arrange chicken pieces on top, sprinkle all the spices, salt and mint over them. Cover with a lid, place over low heat and cook gently 20 minutes until onions and chicken have released their own cooking liquid. Stir thoroughly to combine all ingredients and stir in the yoghurt. Cover pan and continue to cook gently for another 20 minutes. Add chopped tomatoes and ghee. Cook the mixture, stirring frequently until tomatoes are reduced to a pulp. Cover closely and cook very gently 25–30 minutes until chicken is tender and sauce is thickened. Serve sprinkled with chopped coriander and slivered almonds.

Spicy Pineapple and Coconut Curry

1 small ripe pineapple, peeled and cut lengthwise in quarters,
    core removed, then cut in bite-sized pieces
1 small onion, chopped
1 tablespoon ghee (see *ghee*)
1 clove garlic, crushed
2 green cardamoms
2 whole cloves
2 1-inch pieces stick cinnamon
1 teaspoon cumin seeds
2 teaspoons ground coriander
salt to taste
chili powder to taste
8oz thick coconut milk (see coconut milk)

Heat *ghee,* add onion, garlic and whole spices and stir-fry to a golden
color. Add ground coriander, salt, chili powder and stir-fry another few
minutes to cook the spices. Reduce heat, add pineapple and stir well
to coat the pieces. Stir in coconut milk and simmer, uncovered 3–4
minutes until pineapple is just tender and sauce has thickened.

Saffron Chicken

2½ pound chicken, cut into eight pieces
2 large onions, chopped
small piece fresh gingerroot, chopped fine
1 fresh red or green chili pepper, seeded and finely chopped
small pinch saffron, infused in a teaspoon of water
3 tablespoons clarified butter (see *ghee*)
1 tablespoon St. Kitts curry powder (see West Indian curry powder)
salt and pepper to taste
1¼ cups coconut milk (see coconut milk)

Heat *ghee* in heavy saucepan and fry chicken in it until golden brown, then drain on heavy paper. Stir-fry the onion and ginger in remaining *ghee* until golden, add all the spices plus salt and pepper and stir fry just a few minutes. Stir in coconut milk and return chicken pieces to pan. Heat through, cover pan and reduce heat, simmer until chicken is tender, about 45 minutes.

From Hawaiian Cook Book a menu for a
Curry Luncheon attributed to Mrs. Gartley:

This luncheon is essentially Hawaiian, easy to serve and especially appropriate for visitors from the mainland.

First course — Tomato salad.
Second Course — Curry, with rice and accompaniments.
Fruit sherbet, coffee, cake.

The tomatoes should be large red ones. Scald and remove skin, scoop out the center and set on ice. Just before serving, set on a lettuce leaf and fill with the following mixture: Chopped Hawaiian celery, a little sweet pickle, a few walnuts, a little onion juice mixed with a good mayonnaise.

The curry can be fish, lobster, chicken, rabbit, lamb or mutton. A good curry sauce will be found on page (00)*. The accompaniments are steamed rice, served in a separate dish, the following five served in the Chinese dish made specially for the purpose: Guava jelly or quartered limes, chopped hard-boiled eggs, chutney, chopped peanuts, fresh grated coconut. The fruit sherbet should be made from any Hawaiian fruit in season: Grape, sour-sop, guava, roselle, papaia, mango, orange, fig, strawberry, pineapple or banana.

*as printed, p. 117 Hawaiian Cook Book compiled by the Womans' Society of Central Union Church, Sixth Edition, Honolulu Star-Bulletin, Ltd. 1920

Coconut Water

The clear liquid inside the coconut is often mistaken for coconut milk but is coconut water which is a refreshing drink. After the nut has been husked, pierce two of the eyes and drain out the water. Use a hammer to crack the coconut open.

Coconut Milk

Scrape the white meat out of the cracked coconut, discarding any of the hard, brown rind. Grate the chunks and place the gratings in layers of cheesecloth and wring and squeeze out all the liquid. The first batch of liquid is thick coconut milk. Thin milk is obtained by adding 2 cups of hot water to 1 cup of grated coconut and letting it stand for 30 minutes before wringing it out again.

Coconut Cream

Grate the coconut and add 1 cup of hot milk to 2 cups of grated coconut and let it stand for 30 minutes before wringing it out in layers of cheesecloth.

Note: Fresh frozen coconut milk can be purchased at markets and is rich enough to use as coconut cream or thinned down for less rich recipes. Look for 12 oz. cans, usually where frozen juice concentrates are stocked.

Beverages To Serve With Curry

Indians do not consume beverages with their meals, other than cooled, not iced, water. Fragrant teas are served after a meal with sweetmeats, and are flavored usually with cinnamon, cloves, or citrus peel. Early tribesmen made liquors from rice, palm juice, and cashews (with resultant methyl alcohol poisonings). Moghuls drank wines imported from Portugal and Spain. The British introduced Scotch and it was a favorite beverage to drink with curry.

The spiciness of curry dishes obscures flavor, character, and bouquet of even the most robust wines, however. Indian beer is a good beverage for serving with the spicy foods, while some prefer a tart lemonade. Very dry white Burgundies are acceptable and some of the livlier red wines. Experiment, and offer a selection of beverages to serve with your curry dinners.

My preference is a darker, full bodied lager beer, one that stand up to the fire of the curry. Some people enjoy a gin and tonic with lime as an accompaniment.

Curry Sambals

Side Dishes

Chutneys, several kinds +
Pomegranate seeds
Spiced raisins +
Diced ripe tomato
Minced American parsley
Minced Chinese parsley
    (coriander)
Finely sliced green onions
Diced unpeeled cucumber
Sour pickle relish +
Crumbled chipped beef
    (Bombay duck substitute)
Sliced crystalized ginger
Mandarin orange sections
Thinly sliced radishes
Mint leaves
Pickled mango slices +
Sieved hard-boiled egg
Fresh pineapple chunks
Preserved kumquats +
Chopped black olives
Grated fresh coconut
Crumbled crisp bacon
Chopped salted peanuts
Onion or cucumber relish +
Pickled eggs +
Sliced carambola (star fruit)

Slivered guava rind
Diced fresh bananas
Sliced mountain apple
Lime wedges
Bombay duck +
Deep fried onion rings
Sliced fresh loquats
Lychees
Sauteed bananas
Dal Bhat +
Guava jelly
Cumin seeds
Thin threads of lemon rind
Sesame seeds, roasted
Finely chopped fresh basil
Baked Bananas +
Wetha Lone Kyaw +
Coconut sambal +
Ginger root pickles +
Cucumber-pineapple sambal +
Sauteed green breadfruit +
And
Mounds of long-grain rice +
Beverages, alcoholic or not +
Fragrant teas
Desserts of fresh fruit,
    or fruit sherbet or sorbet

+ see index

Baked Bananas

Peel bananas, cut in half lengthwise and place cut side down in glass baking dish. Sprinkle over them the juice of one orange, 3–4 tablespoons sugar and scant teaspoon cinnamon. Pour over them 2–3 tablespoons melted butter and bake, uncovered in 350 degree oven about an hour. (For 8–10 bananas)

Sauteed Green Breadfruit

To a quart and a half of boiling water, add about 4 cups of pared and diced green breadfruit and scant teaspoon salt. Cook over moderate heat until breadfruit is tender, then drain. In a pan, melt 3–4 tablespoons butter and saute the breadfruit chunks until they are golden, then sprinkle with freshly ground white pepper to taste. (Do not overcook)

Cucumber-Pineapple Sambal

1 small pineapple, peeled and cubed
2 small cucumbers, peeled and cubed
½ cup blanched almonds
½ cup cream
¼ cup lemon juice
salt and pepper

Mix pineapple and cucumber chunks together with almonds. Make a dressing of the cream and lemon juice, season to taste with salt and pepper and pour over the fruit and chill several hours before serving as a side dish with curry.

Coconut Sambal

Chop a small onion very fine, and add it to 1½ cups shredded fresh coconut. Season with salt and chili powder to taste, and bind together with a tablespoon of lemon juice and a tablespoon of warm milk.

Onion Relish

Cut a red onion into very thin slices, separate them into rings and place in a colander and run cold water over them for a few minutes. Drain the onion, put rings into a bowl and toss with the juice of half a lemon and season with salt to taste.

Cucumber Relish

Peel three small cucumbers, cut in half lengthwise, remove any tough seeds and grate the pieces into a bowl. Toss with 1 tablespoon lemon juice and season with salt and pepper to taste.

Bombay Duck

Bombay duck is an Indian delicacy famous for it's aroma. It is a small, gelatinous fish which has been dried, salted and impregnated with asafetida, a gum resin extracted from the roots of certain plants, which smells of garlic or onion and is very pungent. Bombay duck is served toasted and crumbled over curry and can be purchased at shops in Chinatown.

Wetha Lone Kyaw
Fried Pork Balls
Burma

1 pound lean boneless pork, finely chopped
1 medium onion, finely chopped
1 green chili pepper, seeded and finely chopped
small bunch coriander (Chinese parsley), finely chopped
1 clove garlic, crushed
¼ teaspoon turmeric
salt to taste
½ cup all-purpose flour
4 tablespoons vegetable oil

Mix pork, onion, chili, parsley, garlic, turmeric and salt. Roll into walnut-sized balls, coat with flour. Heat oil in frying pan and cook meatballs a few at a time, turning them carefully until they are crisp and golden. Drain on paper, garnish with sprigs of parsley and serve as accompaniment to curry dishes or as an appetizer.

Dal Bhat
Curried lentils

1 pound red lentils (or whatever is available)
2 quarts boiling, salted water
4 yellow onions, thinly sliced
1 cup bacon drippings or clarified butter (see *ghee*)
5–6 tablespoons curry powder (see curry powder recipes)*

Cover lentils with cold water in large bowl and soak overnight. Drain and add them to the boiling water in a pot on the stove, reduce heat and cook for several hours, covered, until tender. Pour off any liquid remaining and press lentils through strainer or ricer.

In large skillet saute onions in fat until lightly browned. Remove onions from pan and set aside. Into remaining fat add the curry powder which has been made into a paste with a small amount of cold water. Cook until bubbly, then add curry mixture to pureed lentils and serve the mixture over mounds of rice and top with the sauteed onions.

*for a hotter version, add crushed chili pepper in addition to the curry powder.

Dal — Madras

Dal is an Indian puree made of chick peas, lentils, dried beans or split peas, soaked, cooked, flavored, and used as a condiment or a thickening agent.

3 tablespoons clarified butter (see *ghee*)
1 large onion, chopped
1 green chili pepper, seeded and chopped
2 cups washed lentils, chick peas, or yellow split peas
5 cups chicken stock or boiling water
1½ teaspoons curry powder (see curry powder recipes)
2 teaspoons mustard seed, crushed
1 tablespoon fresh coriander leaves (Chinese parsley), chopped
salt to taste

Saute onion and pepper in *ghee*. Add dried peas or lentils and the stock and simmer, covered, about an hour until tender. Add the remaining ingredients and mix well and cook an additional 15 minutes. Rub the cooled mixture through a sieve and store it, covered, under refrigeration until served.

Rice

Rice is to the East what wheat is to the West and is the principal food of over half the people in the world. Rice, ancient grain cultivated in paddys in temperate regions of the world, has long been an important part of the diet of many Asian countries such as India, China, Japan, Maylasia, and the Philippines. 95% of it is grown in the Orient while several European and South American countries grow and eat considerable rice. America produces 1% of the world's rice supply and most of it is exported to England. Originally grown in South Carolina, rice is now grown principally in Louisiana, Texas, Arkansas and California.

There are thousands of varieties of rice and they are classified according to grain size; long, extra-long, medium and short, whether white or brown. In India alone there are 200–400 major rice varieties and the world total of different varieties is over 10,000. They are categorized by their length, whether polished or unpolished, raw or par-boiled, and by their translucency, smell, age, quality and price.

Brown rice in its natural state, is unpolished and retaining its bran layers, is more digestible, superior in food value, requires a long cooking time and more water than white rice, and is tastier. One cup raw or brown rice yields 4 cups cooked rice.

White rice has been hulled, polished with talc, chalk, or glucose, pearled by machine, lost vitamin B and protein, requires less water and a shorter cooking time, but is not as nutritious. One cup white uncooked rice yields 3 cups cooked rice.

Converted rice, also called par-boiled rice, comes in long, short, and medium grains and is processed to retain the vitamins and minerals, takes even less cooking time, and one cup yields about 4 cups of cooked rice.

Instant rice, or precooked rice, is milled, cooked and dehydrated. Although it cooks quickly it has less flavor, is not as nutritious and is more expensive than regular white rice and the yield is also less.

There are also varieties of sweet rice such as the Chinese use to make gelatinous sweet pastries, and wild pecan rice and texmati grown in Louisiana and Texas. They are more like brown rice but have a distinct nutty flavor.

Wild rice is not a true rice but the seeds of an aquatic grass native to Wisconsin, Minnesota and Michigan, as well as Canada. It is also commercially cultivated in California.

Short-grain rice, preferred by the Japanese, is sticky when cooked, medium-grain is less so, and long-grain rice, favored by the Indians and Chinese, cooks up to a fluffy, drier grain and in my estimation is the best to serve with curries.

There are so many ways of preparing and cooking rice that I don't recommend one over the other as each person has developed his own special method. Some wash the grains first, others never do. You may lose some of the nutrients in the washing, but it is wise to remove milling and polishing dust if it is present to avoid having a pot of "gluey" rice.

Some cooks soak their rice first from 30 minutes to several hours, others say it spoils the flavor. Soaked rice cooks more quickly, keeps grains separate and absorbs less cooking water. DO NOT add oil or butter to cooking water to prevent sticking. Some cooks add salt to the cooking water, Orientals don't. Then there is the matter of using hot or cold water to start, using a lid on the pot or not, and rinsing or steaming the rice after cooking.

Try anything you like, but my simple recommendations are as follows: select the grain and kind of rice you want, don't soak it, use a large enough pan to allow for expansion and as shallow as possible, measure 1 cup of raw rice to 1 cup of water for white rice, and 1½ cups of water for brown rice. Put the pan on high heat, when water comes to full boil, put the lid on, reduce heat to medium and as water is absorbed (peek briefly) turn to lowest heat setting, leaving lid on until all water is taken up, rice has expanded, and is fully cooked (about 30 minutes all told). Fluff up with fork and serve.

When you get really good at making rice that doesn't burn or stick to the bottom of the pot in a thick, heavy layer, you'll probably know when to lower the heat from high to off and let it steam it's way to being perfectly cooked. Or, get an electric rice cooker, the greatest gadget a kitchen klutz could ever own. I have burned more rice pots than I care to tell you about and I thank the Japanese for inventing the electric rice cooker which allows anyone to cook perfect rice every time, without error or pot scrubbing. Arigato gozai masu!

PICKLED FRUIT

Green Papaya Pickles #1

8 green papayas, peeled and sliced ½-inch thick
4 cups cider vinegar
2 cups brown sugar
1 cup water
4 sticks cinnamon
1 3-inch piece green ginger root, thinly sliced crosswise

Place vinegar, sugar and water into saucepan, add cinnamon and bring to boil, reduce heat and simmer the syrup for 15 minutes. Pack the papaya and ginger slices in sterlized jars and when the syrup has cooled, pour it over the fruit and seal the jars. Let ripen several weeks to allow ginger to flavor the syrup.

Pickled Green Papaya #2

Peel and slice enough green papayas to make 8 cups of diced fruit, set aside. In a saucepan cook 2 cups vinegar, 1 cup sugar, 2 sticks cinnamon and 1 teaspoon whole black peppercorns to boiling. Turn off heat, add fruit to syrup, allow to cool in syrup, then place in sterilized jars and seal.

Dell Neely's Pineapple Pickles

My mother's recipe

6 cups fresh pineapple chunks
2 cups white sugar
1 cup cider vinegar
12 whole cloves
6 2-inch pieces of cinnamon sticks

Put all ingredients into saucepan, bring to boil, turn heat to medium and continue cooking until pineapple turns a clear golden yellow. Pour fruit and syrup into hot, sterilized glass jars and seal. Let jars "ripen" about two weeks so fruit will absorb spices.

Papaya Pickles #3

1½ cups water
1½ cups sugar
¾ cup cider vinegar
½ teaspoon ground white pepper
6 whole cloves
1 stick of cinnamon
3 tablespoons papaya seeds
2 ripe, but firm, papayas; peeled, seeded and cut into ½ inch dice

In a saucepan combine all ingredients, except papaya, and bring to a boil; reduce heat and simmer 15 minutes. Add diced papaya and continue to cook about 45 minutes. Pour fruit and syrup into hot sterilized jars and seal.

Pickled Figs

Wash ripe but firm figs, do not peel. In a large saucepan put 4½ cups sugar and 4 cups vinegar, small handful of whole cloves, several sticks of cinnamon, broken, and a tablespoon black peppercorns and bring mixture to boiling. Add enough figs to float freely in liquid, reduce heat, and continue to simmer until figs are done when pierced with a fork. Remove figs to jars, and continue to boil liquid down to a thicker syrup, then pour over fruit in jars, cap and seal.

Pickled Whole Peaches

2 pounds ripe peaches, not too large
8 cloves
2½ cups white sugar
1 cup cider vinegar
1 cup water
2 small sticks of cinnamon

Pour boiling water over washed peaches in a bowl, let set briefly, pour off water and slip skins off the fruit. Combine sugar and vinegar with water and spices in a pan. Boil, covered, for about 7 minutes. Add peaches, continue boiling gently until they are soft when pierced with a fork, about 20–30 minutes. Pack them into hot sterilized jars and seal. Let the jars "ripen" several weeks before serving.

Watermelon Pickles

Rind of one watermelon
2 cups vinegar
1 cup sugar
1 tablespoon cinnamon
1 tablespoon cloves
1 tablespoon allspice

Remove the red meat portion of melon and pare off the green outside skin as thinly as possible. Cut the white part of the rind into small pieces about one or one and a half inches square. Boil them in water to cover until tender, drain off water and place them in a large bowl.

Put remaining ingredients in a pot and cook until the consistency of heavy syrup, remove from burner and pour syrup over rind in bowl. Return rind and syrup to pan and again bring to a boil. Remove from burner, pack fruit into hot, sterilized jars, pour syrup over fruit, and seal.

NOTE: This recipe makes a dark, spicy, soft pickle and is unlike the clear, crisp one bought commmercially. The syrup is heavy with the spices, which you may choose to strain before pouring it into the jars.

Cantaloupe Pickles*

1 medium, not quite ripe, cantaloupe
4 cups vinegar
2 cups water
2 sticks cinnamon
1 tablespoon whole cloves
1 teaspoon ground mace
4 cups brown sugar

Peel and seed cantaloupe, cut into 1 inch chunks and place in large bowl. In a pot place the vinegar and water with spices tied in a cheesecloth bag and bring to a boil. Pour mixture over the cantaloupe chunks and let it stand overnight. Next day, drain vinegar back into a pan, heat to boiling, add the cantaloupe chunks and the 4 cups of sugar. Return pot to a boil, reduce heat and simmer for 1 hour or until transparent.

Pack the fruit into hot, sterilized jars and boil the juice another 5 minutes to the syrup stage, then pour it over the fruit in the jars and seal.

*What to do when the melon you bought at the market never ripens nicely, is rubbery and tasteless, because it was picked too green. However, it cost me $15 to have my sink drain unplugged, when without thinking, I ground the rind in the disposal after I made these pickles. Beware!

Mango Pickle

9 cups green mango slices
6 cups salt water (1 tablespoon salt to 1 cup water)
9 cups sugar
4½ cups vinegar
½ tablespoon whole cloves
½ tablespoon whole peppercorns
4 bay leaves
4½ cups water

Soak mangoes overnight in sufficient salt water to cover. Drain, add the fresh water and cook until partially tender, about 30 minutes; add spices and vinegar, cook about 15 minutes longer, or until mango slices are tender. Drain mangoes and cook syrup until it is slightly thick. Add mangoes, heat to boiling point, and pack in hot sterile jars. Seal immediately, label, and store in cool place.

Bulletin 77
Hawaii Experiment Station
3rd printing January 1939

Pickled Peach Slices

8 cups skinned and sliced fresh peaches
1 tablespoon whole cloves
3 small sticks of cinnamon
4 cups sugar
2 cups vinegar

Put washed whole peaches in a large bowl, pour boiling water over them and let them set briefly, then pour off the water and slip the skins off and slice the fruit fairly thin. In a pan place the sugar and vinegar with the spices tied up in a cheesecloth bag. Bring to boil and stir to dissolve sugar, then continue to boil for 2 minutes. Add the peaches and simmer gently until the fruit is fairly tender but not turning mushy. Pack into hot sterilized jars with a few of the whole cloves in each jar and fill to top with the hot syrup and seal.

Pickled Pineapple Slices

1 ripe pineapple
2 pounds sugar
2 cups water
4 whole cloves
peel of 1 orange, thinly sliced
a 2 inch stick of cinnamon

Pare and core the pineapple, cut it into thin slices and then into quarters. Combine the sugar, water, spices and orange rind and boil for 10 minutes. Add the pineapple, cook another 10 minutes. Let stand overnight, next morning drain syrup from pineapple into a pan, bring to a boil and then pour over the fruit. Repeat this process for two additional days (three processes in all). The last day, pack the fruit into hot, sterilized jars and seal.

PICKLED VEGETABLES

Herbed Carrot Slices

4 pounds carrots, peeled and thinly sliced
1 teaspoon salt
2⅔ cup white vinegar
2⅔ cup water
3 teaspoons dill seed
1 teaspoon mustard seed
1 teaspoon caraway seed
1 teaspoon celery seed
2 cups white sugar
2 teaspoons rock salt
1 teaspoon crushed and seeded Hawaiian chili pepper

Cook carrot slices with 1 teaspoon salt in very small amount of water until almost tender. Drain and pack the slices into hot sterilized jars and pour over them the hot syrup made by combining all the remaining ingredients in a pan, bringing to a full rolling boil and boiling for 2 minutes. When syrup has covered carrots in the jars, seal them and let ripen for several weeks before serving.

Pickled Carrot Sticks

2 pounds carrots, pared and cut lenthwise into 4-inch sticks
1½ cups cider vinegar
1 cup white sugar
1 tablespoon pickling spices
1 tablespoon salt
1 small piece stick cinnamon

Bring to a boil the vinegar, sugar, salt, and spices in a large pan and boil 5 minutes. Add carrots and cook until just tender, about 10 minutes or so. Pack carrots in sterilized jar and pour boiling liquid over them. Seal and allow to set at least 2 weeks before serving. This recipe will fill a quart jar.

Sweet Carrot Pickle

1 pound carrots, peeled and thinly sliced crosswise
½ teaspoon salt
1 cup white sugar
1½ cups white vinegar
1 tablespoon bottled pickling spices

Cook carrots in small amount of water with the salt until nearly tender. Drain, and set aside. Put sugar and vinegar in pan with spices tied in cheesecloth. Bring mixture to boil and boil gently until juices form a syrup. Add carrots and simmer slowly for 20 minutes. Pack into hot sterilized jars and seal.

Bread and Butter Pickles

12 large cucumbers (do not peel)
6 large onions
1½ pints vinegar
2½ cups sugar
1 teaspoon whole black peppercorns
1 teaspoon celery seed
1 teaspoon mustard seed
1 teaspoon turmeric powder

Slice cucumbers and onions ¼ inch thick and soak overnight in salt water. Drain. Combine vinegar, sugar and spices and bring to a boil. Add cucumbers and onions and cook until tender, 10–12 minutes. Put in sterile jars and seal.

*From Cathedral Cooks, published by the
Library Committee of St. Andrew's Cathedral
Honolulu 1964*

Pickled Nasturtium Seeds

A caper substitute

Use green nasturtium seeds with a short length of stem on each. Lay the seeds in cold, salted water for 2 days (2 tablespoons salt per quart of water). Rinse and lay in fresh cold water for another day.

Drain well and place the seeds in a clean, sterilized glass jar, cover with vinegar which has been heated to the boiling point. Cover tightly and allow to set for a few days. They are an excellent substitute for capers.

Pickled Beets

1 bunch beets
½ cup beet cooking liquid
2 cups white vinegar
1 cup white sugar
1 teaspoon salt
3 tablespoons pickling spices
1 large onion, sliced

Trim beets, leaving root and 1 inch of the top to prevent bleeding. Cook until tender. Drain and save the cooking liquid. Slip off skins, roots, and stems. Slice about ¼-inch thick. Combine the beet liquid, vinegar, sugar, and salt in a large pan. Add spices tied in a cheesecloth bag. Bring to a boil, then add beets and onions. Boil for 8 minutes; remove spices, pack into sterilized jars and seal.

Pickled Hawaiian Onions

This is a very easy method. Peel and wash small locally grown onions and pack in a bowl with salt to cover, overnight. Next day wash and dry them and pack into bottles with 2–3 red chili peppers, several whole cloves and a number of black peppercorns per bottle. To one quart of vinegar in an enameled or stainless pan add 1 cup of brown sugar and bring mix to boiling and pour over the bottled onions. Cool and cap the jars tightly and let "ripen" for a few weeks before serving. These will be very hot — make adjustments on amount of spices and chili peppers to suit your taste.

Pickled Onions

Peel onions and cover with a strong brine in the proportion of ¾ cup of kitchen salt to 1 quart boiling water. Let cool a little before covering onions. Let stay in brine for 24 hours. Pour off brine, wash onions and pack in jars according to size. Put in strips of bell peppers and one or two chili peppers, and cover with boiling vinegar in which has been cooked for about 15 minutes (in a cheesecloth bag) a couple of tablespoons assorted pickling spices and about a teaspoon of mustard seed. To vinegar use sugar in the proportion of one fourth cup to one quart of vinegar. Cool and seal and do not use for at least two weeks.

attributed to Mrs. George Angus

Maui Onion Rings

6 large Maui onions
1 cup sugar
5 teaspoons salt
2 hot red Hawaiian peppers, seeded and minced
ginger root, about 1 inch piece, finely minced
½ teaspoon whole peppercorns
1½ cups white vinegar
½ cup water

Peel onions and slice ¼-inch thick and separate rings. Pack them into sterilized jars, leaving room for plenty of liquid. Combine remaining ingredients in pan and stir over moderately high heat until sugar is dissolved and pour over onion rings in jars. Cover and store in refrigerator.

Green Ginger Root Pickles

1 pound fresh young ginger root, peeled
2 tablespoons salt
1½ cups rice vinegar
1 cup white sugar
½ teaspoon peppercorns, preferably white, but black will do

Wash ginger root and thinly slice and cover with the salt in a bowl. Cover and chill in refrigerator overnight, then rinse off salt and drain in a sieve. In a pan place vinegar, sugar and peppercorns and bring to a full boil, add ginger slices and return to a boil. Remove from burner and when cooled place in covered glass container and refrigerate several days before using. Will keep a few weeks and may be made without peppercorns for a less pungent pickle.

These pickles can also be packed into hot, sterilized jars and refrigerated.

Don'ts for Mothers

Don't try to do two days' work in one; and, in your homemaking, beware lest you become a veritable fiend of neatness.

If work you must, simplify your duties so that they will not prove a weariness to the flesh. Never stand when you can sit down. When waiting at the counter for change, why neglect the stool close at hand? It is only a matter of five minutes, perhaps, but it may be five minutes too long, and then how your poor, tired back rebels! Don't save horse-car fare for the sake of taking home a pound box of candy. It is a foolish woman who will squander her pennies on trash, and walk her legs nearly off to make up the deficit. Don't try to do without your roll and coffee or glass of milk when the luncheon hour arrives, no matter how long and discouraging your shopping list may be.

In short, strive not to be an amateur in the art of caring for yourself, but in the details of life look well to it that they are made subservient to your womanly needs.

These remarks above were wedged in between Pickled Onions and Papaia Cocktails from a cookbook compiled by the Womans' Society of Central Union Church, Honolulu and printed in 1920.

Marinated Mushrooms — No. 1

2 pounds tiny mushrooms, washed and stems removed
1 cup dry white wine
½ cup light vegetable oil
½ cup olive oil
½ cup lemon juice
¼ cup parsley, minced
3 garlic cloves, minced
1 tablespoon brown sugar
2 teaspoons dried thyme leaves
1½ teaspoons salt
½ teaspoon ground black pepper

In pan put all ingredients except mushrooms, simmer, covered for 15 minutes. Add mushrooms and simmer another 8–10 minutes. Remove from heat and cool. Place in sterilized jars, seal and keep in refrigerator for several days before serving.

Marinated Mushrooms — No. 2

2 pounds small, whole mushrooms, washed and stems removed
¾ cup olive oil
½ cup white wine vinegar
1½ cups water
3 bay leaves
1½ teaspoon fennel seed
1 teaspoon thyme
¼ cup parsley, minced
1½ teaspoon salt
½ teaspoon whole peppercorns

In a pan mix the water, oil, and vinegar and bring to a boil, then add the herbs and seasonings. Simmer, covered, for 10–15 minutes. Add the mushrooms and simmer for another 15 minutes. Remove from heat and let the mushrooms cool in the marinade. Place in covered container in refrigerator a few days before serving.

Kijuri Namasu
Japanese Cucumber Relish

3 cups cucumber, thinly sliced
1 teaspoon salt
1 teaspoon grated fresh ginger root
½ cup Japanese rice wine vinegar, or regular white vinegar
2 tablespoons sugar
ajinomoto (msg) very small dash

Leaving some of the green peel on the cucumber, slice it very thinly, place in a bowl, add the salt and let it stand 30–45 minutes. Drain and press off the excess liquid and add the rest of the ingredients to the cucumber. Chill well before serving.

Nice additions are thin slices of black mushrooms, small strips of canned abalone, bits of grated carrot, and pieces of edible seaweed.

Marinated Maui Onions

½ cup olive oil
1 tablespoon salt
½ teaspoon sugar
2 tablespoons lemon juice
2 cups Maui onion, coarsely chopped
½ cup bleu cheese, crumbled

Mix oil, lemon juice, salt and sugar in a cup. Stir in the cheese and pour mixture over the onions, in a bowl. Cover tightly and chill for several days, stir occasionally. Drain off excess oil, serve with small slices of thin rye bread, crackers or with pumpernickel.

Stephanie Burgess

Takuwan

Japanese Pickled Turnips — No. 1

3–4 large turnips, peeled and sliced ¼-inch thick (daikon)
¾ cup white vinegar
1½ cups sugar
3 tablespoons salt
1–2 chili peppers or a dash of cayenne pepper
¼ teaspoon yellow food coloring

Add salt to turnips and let stand overnight. Drain. Combine other ingredients and pour over turnips. Store in refrigerator. Another method calls for first cooking together the vinegar, sugar and salt a few minutes. When liquid is cool, add the sliced turnips and refrigerate.

Takuwan

Japanese Pickled Turnips — No. 2

4–5 average sized turnips, (daikon) peeled and cut into sticks
3 tablespoons salt
1½ cups white sugar
1 cup white vinegar
1 tablespoon chopped fresh ginger root
2 Hawaiian chili peppers, seeded and crushed
¼ teaspoon yellow food coloring

Pour salt over turnip sticks in a large bowl and let stand overnight. Drain next day and pack the sticks into clean, sterilized jars. Combine all other ingredients and pour the mixture over the turnips and seal the jars. Refrigerate for several days before serving.

Kim Chee

Korean Pickled Cabbage

2 pounds cabbage or won bok (celery cabbage)
½ cups Hawaiian salt
4 cups water
2 small, hot, red peppers, minced (Hawaiian chili peppers)
2 cloves garlic, minced
1 teaspoon ginger root, minced
½ teaspoon paprika
1 tablespoon white sugar
¼ teaspoon ajinomoto (msg)

Cut cabbage into 2 inch lengths. Dissolve salt in water and soak cabbage in this brine for 4 hours, then rinse and drain. Add the seasonings to the cabbage, mixing well. Pack into a quart jar, cover loosely and let stand at room temperature for a day or two to "ripen", then refrigerate.

Some adjusting may be needed as you might like this dish milder or hotter, depending on your tastes.

RELISH

Corn Relish

5 ears sweet corn, kernels cut off
1 large onion, chopped
6 tablespoons sugar
½ teaspoon celery seed
1 hot red pepper, seeded and minced
½ teaspoon mustard seed
½ teaspoon salt
1 green bell pepper, chopped
2 cups vinegar
3 tablespoons pimento, minced

Mix all ingredients together in a pan and bring to a boil. Lower heat and continue to simmer about 45 minutes, uncovered. Pack into sterilized jars and seal. Refrigerate after opening.

Beet Relish

1 quart chopped, cooked beets
1 quart chopped, raw cabbage, thinly shredded
2 cups white sugar
1 cup fresh horseradish, grated
1 tablespoon salt
1 teaspoon ground black pepper
½ cup white vinegar

Combine beets, cabbage, sugar, horseradish, salt, and pepper. Pack into sterilized jars and add 2 tablespoons vinegar to each pint jar. Seal and store in a dark, cool place for several weeks before serving. Refrigerate after opening.

Onion Relish

6 large onions, diced
1 large red bell pepper, diced
⅔ cup brown sugar
⅔ cup apple juice
½ cup white wine vinegar
1 tablespoon salt
1 tablespoon prepared horseradish
1 tablespoon salad oil
1 tablespoon prepared mustard, preferably Dijon type

Put all ingredients into a large pan and heat to boiling, reduce heat and simmer, uncovered, 20 to 30 minutes, stirring a few times. Pack into sterilized jars and keep refrigerated. Let stand at least overnight before serving with hamburgers and other meat sandwiches.

Turnip Relish

2 cups finely grated turnip
1 cup finely grated white onion
½ cup white wine vinegar
¼ cup prepared horseradish
3 tablespoons sugar
¾ teaspoon salt

Mix together all ingredients and pack into sterilized jars and seal. Keep refrigerated. Makes a nippy accompaniment to many meat and vegetable dishes.

East India Relish

6 cups onions, chopped
4 cups carrots, peeled, shredded and packed
4 cups green tomatoes, diced and packed
4 cups zuccini, finely chopped
2 cups light corn syrup
2 cups white vinegar
2 tablespoons salt
1 tablespoon ground coriander
2 teaspoon ground ginger
1 teaspoon dry red pepper flakes
½ teaspoon ground cumin

Combine all ingredients in pan, heat to boiling, reduce heat and simmer 5–6 minutes. Spoon into hot, sterilized jars and seal. Let ripen before serving.

Tomato Relish

3# ripe tomatoes, peeled and coarsely chopped
1 cup onions, finely chopped
3 stalks celery, finely chopped
salt
1 tablespoon curry powder
1¼ tablespoons flour
½ teaspoon dry mustard
2½ cups malt vinegar (white, if available)
1½ cups white sugar

Dip tomatoes in boiling water for 30 seconds, slip off skins and chop. Place tomatoes, onions and celery in a bowl, sprinkle liberally with salt, cover, and let stand 24 hours. Mix curry, flour and mustard with a little vinegar to form a paste and set aside. Next day drain vegetables, rinse, drain again, place in a pan and heat, but not boil, and simmer for 5 minutes.
Dissolve the sugar in the remaining vinegar and add to the vegetables in pan and simmer about 30 minutes. Add the paste and continue to cook another 3 minutes. Pack into hot, sterilized jar and seal. Let ripen before serving.

Middle Eastern Relish

1 small cucumber, skin on, chopped
½ small red onion, chopped
½ green bell pepper, chopped
1 tomato, chopped
2 tablespoons parsley, chopped
2 tablespoons white vinegar
1 tablespoon olive oil
1 garlic clove, crushed
½ teaspoon sugar
¼ teaspoon salt
dash pepper
1 tablespoon fresh mint, chopped
3 ounces feta cheese, if desired (optional)

Lightly salt the cucumber and let stand in a strainer 1 hour to drain. In a bowl mix all ingredients and let stand, covered and refrigerated overnight before serving.

Sour Pickle Relish

8 good quality, firm dill pickles, sliced crosswise, thinly
1 small can pimentos, sliced thinly
2 cups sugar
1 cup vinegar
1 clove garlic

Boil to a thick syrup the sugar, vinegar and garlic and cool slightly and pour warm syrup over pickles and pimento in a sterilized jar. Seal and refrigerate 24 hours before serving.

Piccalilli

4 pounds green tomatoes, thinly sliced
6 medium onions, thinly sliced
½ cup salt
2 small green bell peppers, chopped
2 cups white sugar
1 pint cider vinegar
2 tablespoons celery seeds
2 tablespoons mustard seeds
1 tablespoon whole cloves
1 teaspoon peppercorns
2–2" sticks cinnamon, broken

In large bowl place layers of tomatoes and onions, sprinkled with the salt. Cover and let stand in cool place overnight. Next day, drain and rinse well with cold water, drain again. Place mixture in saucepan, add peppers, sugar, vinegar and celery and mustard seeds. Tie the remaining spices in a cheesecloth bag and add to the pan. Stir until sugar dissolves, place on burner and bring to the boil and boil rapidly 15 minutes. Remove spice bag, spoon piccalilli into hot sterilized jars and seal. Let stand several weeks before using.

Cranberry Relish No. 1

1 pound bag raw cranberries
2 oranges, quartered, seeded, rind left on
1 cup sugar
1 cup walnuts

Grind all of the above in blender or food processor to a coarse consistency. Pack into sterilized jars and refrigerate.

Cranberry Relish No. 2

1 pound bag raw cranberries
2 apples, peeled and chopped
2 oranges, quartered, seeded, rind left on
1½ cups sugar
1½ ounces cognac or rum

Grind all of the above in blender or food processor to a coarse consistency. Pack into sterilized jars and refrigerate.
Buy bags of cranberries when the local markets bring them in for the holiday season and keep them in your freezer to use throughout the year. They freeze well and keep a long time. They can be ground in a frozen state; no need to thaw them first.

MARMALADE

Preserved Kumquats

1 pound fresh kumquats
2 cups sugar
3 tablespoons light corn syrup
2 cups water

Wash and thoroughly clean the fruit and prick each kumquat with a darning needle (or kitchen skewer) for better penetration of syrup. Cover them well with cold water and boil them until they are tender, then drain off liquid. Make a syrup of the sugar, corn syrup and water and heat it until the sugar is dissolved. Add the kumquats and cook until the fruit is transparent (218 degrees on a candy thermometer). Add, if necessary, a little boiling water to maintain this temperature until the fruit is clear. Let them stand in the liquid for 24 hours, weighting them down under the syrup with a heavy plate. Then cook to 224 degrees, pour into hot, sterilized jars and seal.

From the collection of Mrs. George Angus
Written on a penny postcard.

Palace Hotel Marmalade

6 pounds of carrots
2 large grapefruit
4 lemons
2 oranges
5 pounds of sugar

Pare and thinly slice carrots, place in pan with water to cover, and cook until very tender, then drain. Mash them or sieve or puree them. Extract juice from citrus fruit and add to the carrots. Barely cover the citrus rinds with water, boil gently about 15 minutes. Drain the rinds and add the cooking water to the carrots also. Cool the rinds, cut them in narrow strips and add to the carrots. Add the sugar, stir once, and let the pot stand overnight. Next day boil for 30 minutes to desired consistency and seal in sterilized jars.

(brought back by a traveler to San Francisco)

Maui Onion Marmalade

3 pounds Maui onions, coarsely chopped
6 tablespoons corn oil
1 cup white sugar
1 tablespoon honey
2 teaspoons salt
1 cup dry white wine
¾ cup white-wine vinegar
½ teaspoon allspice
2 teaspoons ground white pepper

Saute the onions in the oil, stirring, for 2–3 minutes. Add the sugar, honey, salt and pepper and cook, covered, over low heat about 30 minutes, stirring occasionally. Add the wine, vinegar and allspice and bring mixture to a boil. Simmer, uncovered, for another 30 minutes, stirring until thickened. Pack into hot sterilized jars and seal.

Presto Papaya Jam

This jam recipe is quick, easy, tasty, and the only one I've ever had success with. Enjoy!
2 ripe papayas
8 ounce can crushed unsweetened pineapple, undrained
1 teaspoon lime juice

Halve, seed, and peel papayas and cut into small cubes to yield 2 cups of fruit. In a saucepan bring papaya and pineapple just to a boil, then stir in lime juice, remove from heat and cool. Store in covered containers in refrigerator for as long as a few weeks or in freezer for a few months. It has a short life but is so easy to make.

Punahou School Papaya Marmalade

10 cups sliced firm ripe papaya
1 cup fresh shredded pineapple
½ cup orange juice
½ cup lemon juice
Grated rind of 1 orange and 2 lemons
3 tablespoons grated green ginger root
1 cup sugar for each cup of cooked fruit

Combine all ingredients except sugar; boil for 30 minutes. Measure cooked fruit and add equal measure of sugar. Cook together for 30 minutes, stirring frequently to prevent burning. When done, pour mixture into hot sterilized jars and seal.

Cucumber Marmalade

1½ to 2 pounds cucumbers, peeled, finely chopped
    and measuring 2 cups
⅓ cup fresh lemon juice
2 tablespoons grated lemon rind
4 cups white sugar
1 6 oz. packet liquid fruit pectin

Into saucepan put the chopped cucumber and lemon juice and rind. Add sugar, mix well, and bring to full rolling boil over high heat. Boil hard for a full minute, stirring constantly. Remove from heat, stir in pectin immediately, Skim off foam and ladle quickly into hot sterilized jars and seal. Serve as a condiment to roast meat, particularly lamb and pork.

Chinese Orange
(Calamondin) Marmalade

Wash fruit, cut them in half, remove seeds and squeeze the juice out. Coarsely chop the fruit or grind in food processor briefly to cut up the pulp and skins. For one cup of juice add three cups of water. Add the chopped skins and pulp to the juice in a large saucepan and let stand for 12 hours, then boil for 20 minutes. Let it stand again for 12 hours and the next day boil again for 20 minutes, then let stand another 12 hours. On the third day, measure 1½ cups of sugar for each cup of mixture and boil together until jelled, then seal in hot, sterilized jar. This makes a very tart marmalade.

Ginger Marmalade

3 oranges
1 lemon
1½ cups water
5 cups white sugar
1 packet liquid fruit pectin
½ teaspoon baking soda
1 6-oz. box candied, crystallized ginger, chopped

Peel oranges and lemon, slicing rind very thin or process in blender. Chop fruit, saving juices, set aside. In saucepan put the water and soda, add the rinds and bring to a boil, lower heat, cover and simmer for 20 minutes, stirring often. Now add fruit and juices, cover and simmer another 10 minutes. Measure the pulp, using 3½ cups of it, put it into another saucepan, add the sugar and ginger and boil it hard for a full minute. Add the pectin and cook one more minute, stirring constantly. Remove from heat, pour into hot sterilized jars and seal.

Keeaumoku Street Guava Marmalade

Jeanie Towill

Peel about 20-25 large (about the size of a lemon) ripe but firm, yellow guavas with a vegetable parer. Cut them in half, scoop out seeds and pulp into a pot. Thinly slice the guava shells and place them in a separate pot. Cover both with just enough water to cover and cook gently until slices are soft and seeds and pulp are mushy. Do not drain liquid from the sliced shells. Sieve the pulp through a strainer, discarding seeds, reserving puree.

Slice 2 lemons, cut in fourths, remove seeds and place in pot with just enough water to cover and simmer gently until soft, but do not drain off liquid.

Combine the guava slices, lemon slices and sieved pulp and measure the amount. Add a scant cup of sugar for each cup of fruit, plus 4 sticks of cinnamon broken in half. Cook the mixture over medium-high heat, stirring frequently to prevent scorching, until it thickens. Pour into hot, sterilized jars and seal.

Note: The combined mixtures, after the first cooking, without the sugar and spices can be refrigerated for up to a week or frozen to be cooked at a later time.

Guava Marmalade

4 pounds whole ripe guavas (48–50 medium-sized)
6 cups sugar
2 cups water
¼ cup lemon slices, thinly sliced and cut in half
1½ teaspoons grated green ginger root (or more)

Wash fruit, remove blossom end, cut fruit into halves and remove soft inner pulp and seeds with a spoon. Cut the rinds into fairly thin strips, cover with the sugar and water and let stand for 3-4 hours. Place the mixture in a large enough pot, add the grated ginger root and lemon slices and bring to boil and continue cooking just until the syrup thickens slightly, but not to the jelly stage. Pour into hot, sterilized jars and seal at once.

Hawaii Agriculture Experiment
Station Bulletin No. 77

Hot Pepper Jelly

2 cups ground green or red bell peppers*
¼ cup seeded and ground red Hawaiian chili peppers
6½ cups white sugar
1½ cups cider vinegar
6 ounces Certo –liquid fruit pectin (there are 2–3 ounce packets
    per box)

Core, seed and chunk the bell peppers and grind them with seeded hot chilis in a blender, using caution in handling of the chilis as stated elsewhere in this book. Place sugar and vinegar in large pan and bring to full rolling boil, remove from burner and let stand, uncovered for 20 minutes. Add peppers to pan, return pot to burner and bring to boil again and continue to cook another 2 minutes, boiling rapidly. Remove from burner, add the pectin and stir the pot for a full 5 minutes. Pour jelly into hot sterilized jars and seal.

*This recipe is adaptable to whatever peppers you can find in the markets. Green peppers and green jalapeno peppers make a clear, light amber colored jelly and ripe red peppers with Hawaiian or other hot red chilis makes a glorious pinky-orange jelly, beautiful to behold! Serve with meats such as lamb, beef, ham, or as a delectable pupu when served atop cream cheese on crackers. Or as a nippy accompaniment to omelettes, and in cold turkey sandwiches.

MISCELLANEOUS BONUS

Spiced Raisins

2½ cups raisins
2 cups water
1½ cups sugar
¾ cup white vinegar
2 cinnamon sticks
1 teaspoon whole allspice
1 teaspoon whole cloves

Combine raisins and water in a saucepan and bring to boil; cover, reduce heat and simmer 5 minutes. Add sugar, vinegar and spices and continue to simmer, uncovered, for 20 minutes or until the raisins are tender and liquid is reduced. Pour into hot, sterilized jars or cool and store in covered container in refrigerator.

Easy and Quick Spiced Fruit

Using canned peaches, apricots, or pears

Make a syrup of ½ cup sugar and ½ cup cider vinegar and boil for 15 minutes. Add *drained* fruit from a large (28 oz) can and simmer over moderately low heat for another 7–10 minutes. Pour into large bowl, let cool, then refrigerate, covered. Use with roasted meat or with other fruit for a simple dessert.

If you wish the fruit spicier, add a cinnamon stick or several dried cloves to the pot as it simmers.

Mango Seed

40 green mangoes
½ cup medium ground salt or Hawaiian rock salt
2 pounds dark brown sugar
1½ cups light corn syrup
1 teaspoon red food coloring
2 teaspoons kum chow mut (Chinese allspice)*
1 teaspoon heong liu fun (Chinese 5–spice powder)**

Peel green mangoes, cut through the young seeds into halves or fourths, removing inner kernel only. Place the pieces in a large glass or crockery bowl, sprinkle well with salt and let stand overnight. Next day, place the pieces on racks, one layer deep, in shallow pans and dry in a 300 degree oven for 3½ hours with the door open at broil position, or dry them in the sun for about 4 days.

Rinse the dried mangoes, place them in a large saucepan and add water just to cover. Cook for 10 minutes or longer if mangoes are well dried. Drain, add sugar, syrup, coloring and spices. Cook for about 30 minutes stirring occasionally. Cool, then store in sterilized jars.

Several amendments to the recipe are: substituting dark corn syrup for light, adding several teaspoons thick Chinese shoyu, and using powdered licorice for yet another taste. It's all up to you.

*can be purchased at shops in Chinatown
* recipe follows

Chinese Five-Spice Powder

2 tablespoons cracked black peppercorns, preferably
    Szechuan pepper
12 3-inch sticks whole cinnamon
12 whole star anise
30 whole cloves
2 tablespoons fennel seeds

Whirl all ingredients to a powder in electric grinder or blender. Use to enhance flavor of meat and poultry but must be used sparingly, about ½ teaspoon per pound of meat. Store in glass container with tight lid in a cool, dark, dry place.

Papaya Marinade

1 papaya, peeled, seeded and chopped
½ cup orange juice
¼ cup vegetable oil
2 tablespoons lemon juice
1 tablespoon curry powder, preferably Madras type
2 teaspoons salt

Put all above ingredients into blender or food processor and puree. Use puree to marinate chicken or pork. Refrigerate marinated meat overnight before grilling.

Tomato Conserve

2 lemons
1 pint diced tart apples
4 cups sugar
1 quart ripe tomatoes
1 cup shredded pineapple, canned and drained

Cut lemons in thin slices, cover with water and cook until tender. Add peeled and quartered tomatoes, apples, pineapple and sugar. Cook until thick and clear. Put in jars, seal and store until ready to use.

*From Cathedral Cooks published by the
Library Commitee of St. Andrew's Cathedral
Honolulu 1964*

Tomato Catsup

8 quarts ripe tomatoes, peeled and quartered
3 onions, quartered
1 teaspoon hot red pepper or 2 dried red peppers
1 bayleaf
1 tablespoon whole allspice
1 clove garlic, peeled
1 stick cinnamon
2 cups vinegar
½ cup sugar
1 tablespoon celery salt

Put small batches of quartered tomatoes in jar of electric blender and blend until pureed and smooth. Pour into strainer over large bowl and repeat grinding and straining. Add quartered onions to last batch of tomatoes and grind together. Pour through strainer. Put 4 quarts of puree in pan, tie spices in cheesecloth bag and add to pan and bring contents to boiling, stirring constantly. Reduce heat, boil gently 1 hour or until mixture has thickened. Skim off foam and pour into hot sterilized jars or bottles.

Quickie Barbecue Relish

1 cup tomato catsup
½ cup onion, grated
¼ cup green bell pepper, finely chopped
¼ cup green stuffed olives, finely chopped
½ teaspoon oregano

Combine all ingredients and let stand, covered and refrigerated at least 24 hours before serving with barbecued ribs.

Pickled Eggs No. 1

18 small eggs
1 quart vinegar
1 tablespoon black peppercorns
1 teaspoon fresh ginger root, grated
1 teaspoon whole allspice

Hard boil eggs for 15 minutes and cool immediately in cold water. Peel shells and put eggs in wide mouth jars. Boil peppercorns, ginger and allspice in vinegar for 10 minutes, strain and pour while hot over the eggs. Let cool, then seal and refrigerate. Ready to serve in 2 weeks time.

Pickled Eggs No. 2

12 eggs
4 cups malt vinegar
3 cinnamon sticks
10 whole cloves
2 teaspoons whole allspice
10 peppercorns
1 chili pepper, finely chopped

Place eggs in pan with cold water to cover and add 1 teaspoon vinegar. Bring to boil, cook 10 minutes, then set eggs in bowl of cold water, peel them, and place them in sterilized wide-mouth jars. Heat the vinegar and spices just to a boil and let the mixture steep, off the burner, to 2 hours, then pour it over the eggs in the jars and seal. Let set for 2 weeks before serving.

The next time you're feeling poorly, consider these cures!

Burnt Flour Custard

One pint milk, 1 egg well beaten, 4 lumps of cube sugar, 1 pinch of salt, 1 tablespoon of burnt flour. Boil the milk; wet the flour with cold milk and the egg; stir into the boiling milk and strain. Excellent for the sick.

Toast Water

Toast 3 slices of stale bread a very dark brown, but do not burn. Put into a pitcher and pour over them a quart of boiling water; cover closely and let it stand on the ice to cool. Strain. It is good for nausea from diarrhoea.

From Hawaiian Cook Book, under the heading of Invalid Cookery
Compiled by the Women's Society of Central Union Church
Honolulu 1920

INDEX

NOTES

NOTES

NOTES

NOTES

NOTES

NOTES

NOTES